With Best Wishes for a
Rapid Recovery to Leo
from Lavina
and Lewis

January 6, 1984

Morning Chores

Morning Chores

HADLEY READ

Illustrations by Lydia Rosier

and Other Times Remembered

University of Illinois Press Urbana Chicago London

Second printing, 1978

© 1977 by the Board of Trustees of the University of Illinois
Manufactured in the United States of America

To Lillian and Benjamin
   whom we called Mom and Dad

Let Me Explain

So many have written so much
about how it was in rural America
        in the late 20's and early 30's
as the nation entered
the second half of its second century.

How it was
when a young man named Lindy
        flew to Paris all alone
and an older man named Coolidge
        said he chose not to run
and a statesman named Hoover was nominated
        promising prosperity forever for everyone.

How it was
        in such a little while
with the crash of 1929
and the world coming apart
        in the Great Depression.

How it was
when the bottom fell out of land prices
and farmers sold corn for seven cents a bushel
and fat steers brought only three cents a pound
                        on the Chicago market
and a wagonload of oats
        wouldn't buy a pair of shoes.

How it was
when the drouth came
        and the grasshoppers
                and the dust storms
and the only thing left was faith and hope
                and hardly enough of that.

How it was finally
when rural America pulled itself out of the mud
and tractor power replaced horse power
and long wire strands on tall poles
brought electricity down country roads
       to light houses
            and pump water
                 and turn feed mills.

When I grew older
I learned from books the way it was.
But all the time when I was growing up
and moving through the years from ten to teens
that's not the way it was at all.

That's why I think it's right
to tell you how it really was
when I was growing up a country boy—
       at least in ways that I recall.

Contents

Our World

Our world then
      when I was growing up.
Seven of us.
To share the house and farm the land.
To talk at night
      about those things that families talk about.

I Can Remember

The house was there
        where it always was
        and should have been
when I returned after thirty years.
Waiting for me.
Wondering when I would come
        to fix the screen door.

More alone now and naked.
Self-conscious with the trees gone—
trees that once hid its plainness
                        and its age.
The big pine gone.
Close friend.
Solitary sentinel by the front porch.
Sheltering a family of hoot owls
                        in summer.
Holding back the blustering winds
                        in winter.

Gone, too, the elm nearer the road
                        fragile and fast growing.
Victim of too many ice storms
that broke its body and its spirit.
Only a blank space east of the house
        where the mulberry tree had been.
It furnished summer fruit for robins
and for small boys who climbed its branches
        to see if the pirates were coming.
Felled by the new owner's axe
                        the neighbors said.
The missus didn't like mulberries anyway.
That same axe
        chopped down the box elder trees
        that shaded the back yard on summer days.

So the house was alone now
        leaning ever so slightly to the east.
Submitting at last to age
        and the winds of winter.

Denied, too, the company of the orchard.
Its trees succumbed years ago to benign neglect.
            before that phrase had special meaning.

The wash house was still standing
            down the walk from the back porch.
So was the coal house
            twelve steps beyond.
Neither used for its original purpose.
But little point in tearing them down now.
That could wait
until later in the summer anyway.
Then the eyesore of an old house would come down
            and be gotten rid of once and for all.

The new house was almost finished
                        ranch style and brick veneer
invading the area east of the house
where the maple trees once were
and where we pitched horseshoes on summer nights.
For a little while longer
the old house would be where it always was
            and where it was supposed to be.

But how could time have moved the barn
            so much closer to the house
            and the crib so much closer to the barn?
Or did it just seem that way
now that corn was planted
            where the feedlots used to be?
A machine shed squatted sullenly
            there to the north
            where once the milk house stood.
No need for a milk house now
            when no cows are milked.
No need for a windmill
            or a water tank for that matter
            or a hog house or a pole-type barn.
Been no livestock on the place they said
                        since just before the war.

4

The new folks allowed as how
        that old house served them well
        since they bought the place in forty-two.
Oh, they'd made some changes here and there.
Perhaps I'd like to see.
No. Thanks anyway.
I could remember the way it was
        when I was growing up
                and my tomorrows were forever.

The Way It Really Was

You've read about our house a hundred times.
Ones like it anyway.
Virtues glowingly described in Sunday ads.
Fiction writers selling quiet rural lives
              to those grown weary of the city.

Spacious country home, those ads will say.
Nestled in the heartland of America
              where air is pure and spirits free.
Ideal for growing family.
Come take the tour, they tease.

Pause first upon the gracious patio
              and let the breeze caress your brow.
Now enter level one and see the way
              the rooms are planned to fit your needs.

The utility room is first
              convenient and trouble free.
And then the multi-purpose kitchen
              waiting for a woman's touch.
From there into the family room
                            so quaint
              and yet with such an atmosphere of charm.
The living room you won't believe
              until you see it for yourself.
Two bedrooms, then, complete the plan.
Six rooms in all.
But there is more.
Two stairways lead up to the second floor.
There you'll find
              each with its own design
four cozy bedrooms tucked away
              just right for quiet, peaceful sleep.
Now step outside again and note how cleverly
two tiny separate houses camouflage facilities
for washing clothes and storing fuel you'll need.

I know that's how the ad would read
if written for the *Tribune* or the *Times*
              or even for the *News-Gazette*.

6

A lot of fancy words and promises.
Not really lies
and yet
not like it was when I was growing up.
So let me tell how I recall our house
the way it was.

The Back Porch

First off
our neighbors would have scoffed
if we had ever had the nerve
to call our plain back porch a gracious patio.
And served us right.

No fancy thing at best, that porch.
Unpainted six-inch boards
       fitted tongue and groove
formed a platform twelve feet square I'd guess.
A cover for the cistern underneath.
Transition point from house to yard
       or yard to house as case might be.
But more than that.
A special kind of place when one looks back.

A place where at the edge
       you scraped your muddy overshoes
       when coming in from doing chores.
A place to sit and wince with pain
       when Mom poured kerosene on cuts we got
       from going barefoot in the rain.
A place to rest when work was done
       and listen to the hired man
       tell of the fun he had when he was young.
A place to make a kite in spring
       to carve a pumpkin in the fall
       to watch the stars on summer nights
       and marvel at the wonder of it all.

We never could have done those things
if we had called that place a gracious patio.

The Little Kitchen

The utility room is first,
    the ad might read.
An ad designed to sell a house
    to someone from the city.
I concede we could have called it that.
We never did.
Family, friends, and even strangers
                when they came
    knew that room for what it was
    and called it by its proper name—
                the little kitchen.
I don't know why the name for sure
    and no one bothered to explain.
I guess I never asked when I was growing up
    although I knew the room
    was seldom used for kitchen tasks.
A giant walk-through hallway
          first of all I'd say.
Some eight feet wide or so and twice as long.
Six steps took you through from back-porch door.

When winter came
we'd play a daily game along one wall.
We'd try to find an unencumbered hook or peg
    and there we'd hang a corduroy coat perhaps
    a fleece-lined mackinaw
    a cap with flaps
    an extra pair of overalls
    and other clothes like that.

And then we'd stand there at the corner sink
          to wash our face and hands.
Cool water flowing on command from cistern pump.
Soft, fresh-smelling when it came
    except in August when it didn't rain
    or in the winter with too little snow
    or when a mouse plunged to a watery grave
    in frightened flight from some imagined foe.
It's true we could detect a musty odor for a time.

Then Dad would lift the porch
          and sprinkle in some lime.
I must explain.
There was no problem actually.
We never drank the cistern water anyway
          coming as it did from summer rain
                    and melted winter snow.
The tin pail on the stand beside the sink
          contained the water that we drank.
We pumped it daily from the well beside the house.
Pure as any water you could find
          or just about I think.

The roller towel was there
          underneath the mirror on the wall
handy for us all to use three times a day.

The kitchen cabinet I guess
          preserved the room's identity and name.
It was the only piece of furniture
          the little kitchen claimed.
In any case
it served its purpose more or less
          with bins for flour, salt, and sugar
          drawers for knives and stirring spoons
          shelves for spices of all kinds
          and storage cupboards underneath.

The counter top
          if not too loaded down with stuff
          like broken skates and husking pegs
          and wind-torn kites and rabbit skins
          and pocket knives with rusty blades
                    and other special, vital things
might now and then be used by Mom
          for mixing cakes or kneading bread
          or filling mason jars with jam.

How unfair, in spite of what I've said so far,
to see the little kitchen only as the place
where clothes were hung and faces washed
and things for baking stored away
                    from mice and rats.

It was much more than that.

Where else but in the little kitchen
could boys bring newborn lambs
                              deserted by their mothers
or take a bath on winter nights
or grind the freshly butchered sausage meat
or build the biggest kite
                              or play with little kittens?
Where else
would there be room to put a wooden box
        that held all sorts of wondrous things
        like two left-footed skates
        a slingshot arch or broken top
        four balls of string
        the stone I got from Uncle Chuck
                who said it was a meteorite
        a once-used robin's nest
        a pocket watch that just might work some day?

Well anyway
that's what our little kitchen was.

The Big Kitchen

True enough the phrase
      large multi-purpose kitchen
but not in ways you might perceive
      the meaning in your mind.
With words like that to tantalize
one might expect to find
      a sweep of gleaming counter tops
      long rows of handsome cupboards
                made of oak
      push-button stove with fridge to match
      all styled to harmonize
             with cozy breakfast nook.
That's how one sees those things
      in all the decorating books
      but not the way it was of course.

Now looking back
if there had been those wondrous things
would they have made the morning mist
          more beautiful to see
or added anything at all
      to laughing talk at supper time
      or living free
      or watching leaves turn golden
          in the fall?
Would washing dishes by machine
have left as many memories
as nightly arguments among us kids
      about who would wash
      and who would dry
      and who would put away?
Would handsome homemade cupboards
         by themselves
compete in memory
with all the things you hoped to find
      on pantry shelves?

Our multi-purpose kitchen was a stage
on which we played our many roles
      of growing up.

The house lights dim.
The music fades.
The curtain rises to reveal
        the setting for life's drama
        that was real.

On the left
the cook stove dominates the scene.
Majestic cast-iron queen.
She feeds on cobs and dusty coal
                        or anything that burns
depositing below the ashes of her greed.
Broad-beamed and pinkish grey when hot
her surface holds more skillets, pans, and pots
than any of the modern kind one finds today.
Underneath that polished top
a baking oven big enough to hold at once
a turkey—twenty pounds at least—
six loaves of bread, three apple pies
and other makings for the feast we'll have
when Christmas comes, or at Thanksgiving time.
Two warming ovens up above
designed to keep food warm I know
but used instead
to dry out stocking caps, wool scarves
and mittens soaking wet from playing in the snow.

Oblong and made of pine
the oilcloth-covered kitchen table
lays claim to center stage.
It's big enough to seat eight comfortably
or nine if weekday company stops by
                        or extra hands are hired on
                        to help at harvest time.
The clock shelf dominates the wall behind.
An eight-inch ledge
        some five feet long or more.
A single stained and varnished board
that holds a hoard of treasures
                        six feet from the floor.
How come the name?

Years before my race with life began
a clock did claim the center of the shelf
                    its rightful place.
An eight-day round-faced friend
that for a while would tell the time
but never did chime on the hour
                    the way we knew it should.
One day it fell and smashed to smithereens.
And after that
we took it to the attic up the stairs.
It was too good a friend to throw away.
Somehow the shelf retained its given name.
Its honest purpose didn't change.
It was from earliest days
the place to store most anything you'd need.
A safety pin, a spool of thread, a pot of paste
          that might be used for making kites.
A magic ring, a leather strap.
A special piece of real strong cord
                    for making gopher traps.
A deck of cards, a candy cane.
Two quarters and a dime
               to pay the ice man when he came.
A Tom Mix badge, a bill of sale.
All letters since December
                    delivered in the mail.
A mouthpiece for a bugle.
Two feathers for a hat.
A fountain pen that seldom worked.
A dime-store compass pointing north.
A ladyfinger firecracker
                    left over from the Fourth.
All that and more
in neatly ordered chaos on the shelf.

A little to the right, beside the cellar door
the wooden box there on the wall
contained the modern wonder of its time—
                    the hand-cranked telephone.
It tied our home by talking wire

to all the other homes along the party line.
Underneath hung from a hook
the phone book listed numbers we could call
                    by ringing Central.
We hardly ever used that book.
Central was a friendly voice
whose major claim to fame was knowing every time
the proper way to ring on any party line.
The only trouble came
when she took sick a day or two
and someone strange
took over Central for the phone exchange.
That didn't happen often—
            maybe once or twice a year.
Central liked to hear the news
            that flowed from everywhere
                    into her tiny room.
It's just as well she did.
How else could she tell those who called
about the hail that fell just south of town?
And how else would she know
about how well the Davis boy was getting on—
the one who had the fever really bad
                    a week or so ago?
Once having seen the magic wonders
            of a rural party line
we weren't surprised in later years
to find how easily a man on earth
        could talk with others on the moon.

The Pantry

The kitchen pantry took the place
     of handsome cupboards on the wall.
A shelf-lined walk-in sort of space.
Rather small but neatly stocked
     with all those things a kitchen needs.

One shelf reserved for stacks of plates
     cups and saucers
     water glasses
     big round bowls and serving platters
     knives and forks
     spoons and ladles
     and other things to set the table.
Another just as handy
     for flour bins and coffee cans
     plus tins to hold the fresh-baked bread
     and cookies from the oven.
The shelf above held row on row
     of canned fruit from the orchard.
Glass mason jars filled to the brim
     with plums and pears and applesauce
     and cherries picked full ripe and red
     to show the robins who was boss.
There were other things on other shelves.
Canned beef and pork
     a crock of lard
     dried peas and beans
     a tin of tea
     glasses filled with jams and jellies
     pickle relish
     sorghum in a gallon pail
     honey in another
     potatoes needed for a week
        brought up from the cellar.

Pantries lost their place for quite a time
             in modern home design.
Now I see they're coming back
     and that makes sense to me.

The Family Room

The family room so quaint
      with such an atmosphere of charm—
That's what the ad might say.
No harm in that.
In fact
the words contain a bit of truth.
But all the same
we never saw the reason
      to give the room a fancy name.
It simply was the place we were
when we were in the house
      regardless of the season.

On winter nights
the round pot-bellied stove
      became my warmest friend.
I'd pull my chair up close
and read about the Rover Boys
      or maybe Rin-Tin-Tin
or do next day's arithmetic
or simply sit in reverie
      and watch the glowing coals.
On other winter nights
the round oak table lighted by Alladin's lamp
      became the center of my universe.
I'd sit and work a jigsaw puzzle
      until it formed a picture of the sea.
I'd watch while Mom sewed patches on my overalls
      or cut a patterned piece of cloth
      to make an apron or a dress.

In spring
the room took on a different personality.
More open now and free.
The stove no longer there.
Its corner place reclaimed
      by Grandpa's rocking chair.
Front door unsealed and open to the breeze
      gave access to the porch

and there we'd watch a thunderstorm
        come rumbling from the south.
Seed catalogues from Henry Field and Earl E. May
shared reading time
        with Sears, Roebuck and Company.
Sometimes I'd stretch out on the floor
        and listen to what programs I could get
        on our beat-up Atwater Kent.

In summer
the place became a dining hall
        the week Mom fed the threshing crew.
The round oak table
        stretching now with all the extra leaves
seated hungry neighbor hands
who Mom said ate like thieves.
On other summer days
the place became a refuge from the heat.
It caught the cooling breeze
from where it came
        to where its destination seemed to be.
Cooler still when evening came
                and chores were done.
We'd sit in quiet dark and talk
about those things we talked about in summer.

The room in fall
reflected all the other seasons of the year
                until first frost appeared.
Then the process of the spring reversed itself
and we prepared the scene for winter once again.

The Parlor

The living room you won't believe
      until you see it for yourself.

Ad writers have a way with words.
They stretch the truth a bit
but seldom far enough to be an outright lie.

The room was not the living room at all.
It was the parlor seen by few
      except on special holidays
      or when some relatives arrived
         to spend a day or two.

Mostly Mom kept closed
those fancy curtained glass-paned doors.
Her reasons we well knew.
It was the only room with carpet on the floor.
What's more,
      the real good furniture was there.
The high-backed mohair davenport.
The leather rocking chair.
The library table made of oak
      with all the faded family pictures
      stuffed into the center drawer.
Two cane-backed chairs with velvet seats
were placed just so
beneath the mirror on the wall.

The parlor was no place to be
      with dirty shoes and faded overalls.
But it was always there
unused, unmussed
and that was good enough for us.

The bedroom off the parlor
was held in strict reserve for company
      or when someone was sick
      or feeling poorly anyway
and didn't feel like being by himself
      like when I had my tonsils out.

Upstairs Bedrooms

It is more fashionable I guess
to speak of bedrooms on the second floor.

We never did.

Instead
         like everybody else we knew
we called them plain old upstairs rooms.
Still do as far as that's concerned.
Four rooms.
None with its own distinct design in fact
                           as intimated by the ad
but each assigned
for all the time that I was growing up.

My sister claimed the corner room
                     a smallish square
with windows facing east and north.
The only one
that had a closet for her clothes.

The bigger one on down the hall
         with windows facing east and south
was called the spare.
Mom saved it for those special guests
or when she hired a girl a month or two
                     to help with all the extra work.

Three boys
         that being Weldon, Bob, and me
all shared the middle room.
Four papered walls
         with doorways leading to the halls.
That's all there was.
No signs of grace
         and yet it was a special place for boys.

Two windows opened to the south
         above the front porch roof.
It was an easy thing on summer nights
to sneak out there and feel the cooling breeze

20

or watch for falling stars
or listen to the sounds of night—
    a far-off barking dog
    soft distant thunder
    a hoot owl in the trees.

The warmest place in winter by a mile.
The stovepipe from the heating stove below
came straight up through the room
    before it made a little jog and disappeared.
We'd lie in bed
    pretending not to hear the call for chores
until the fire below got roaring pretty good.
And then we'd scramble out
to huddle by the stovepipe warm
    before we dressed to face the morning cold.

The bed beside the attic door
was not my favorite sleeping spot.
Especially on those nights when like as not
the hired man would tell his tales of ghosts
he'd heard about
    and claimed Scout's honor to be true.

No matter after that
how hard I tried to think of other things
I knew I heard strange scratching sounds
that had to come from somewhere in the attic.
I'd tell myself it must be mice
                but how could I be sure
even though that very afternoon
I'd shined the flashlight everywhere
looking for the special box I knew was there?
Still—the light was dim.
I could have missed what might have been
that creature waiting to come out
when I was least expecting him.

In any case
it didn't hurt a bit to stay awake
on guard
at least until I fell asleep.

Besides
if I got really scared
I'd make a quick escape into the hall
and down the back hall stairs.

That way
I'd pass right by the hired man's door
          the fourth room on the second floor.
And if need be
I'd yell for help like all get out.

The Cellar

If our house had ghosts
      or other scarey things like vampire bats
      or maniacs with matted hair
      or dreaded one-eyed men from Mars
they'd surely pick the cellar.
It was a better place to hide by far
      than in the attic by my bed.
Nobody ever locked the outside door
that opened on the cellar stairs.

I thought a lot about that possibility
whenever I went down all by myself
      to get potatoes from the bin
      or jars of fruit from shelves
            along the wall.
There was no way a flashlight or a lamp
could let me see what might be there
lurking in some damp far corner of the room.

Like as not
I'd have to put the light down on the floor
to pick the best potatoes of the lot
from those that had begun to sprout.
In that event
I'd whistle really loud
so those upstairs would know that I was safe
and wouldn't get the notion I was scared.

By day the cellar was a different place
especially with the outside door
      left open just a bit—
enough to let in light to make me brave.

Then I could pretend my hiding place a cave
and with my friend Tom Sawyer or Huck Finn
I was secure and safe from those who
sought to steal my hoarded gold from Spain
      or those who called in vain
      to say the time had come
            to hoe the weeds.

The Little Houses

I'm glad
our neighbors never read an ad about our place
that said it had
   facilities for laundering and storing fuel.
That would have made us look like fools.
They'd have thought we'd gone high hat
to use such words as that
to tell about two ordinary buildings
     most everybody had.

The first one was the wash house
   nothing more and nothing less
used as one might guess for washing clothes
   each Monday of the year.
Inside
Mom had her Maytag firmly bolted to the floor
a wash bench with two tubs for catching clothes
   squeezed through the wringer turned by hand
a copper scrub-board hanging on the wall
and underneath
a wash stick she could use for lifting clothes
     from water boiling hot.

The other little house
was just a few steps down the walk.
It got its name
from what the inside bins contained
   one bin for coal and one for cobs
so someone had to choose between the two
and called the place the coal house.
No one bothered to explain just why.
Cob house would have meant the same.

It probably is proper now
to say a word or two
about another little house our family used.
It's been the point of jokes so long
     and that is wrong
because it had a most important role to play.

24

If it were being built today
I guess it would have been renamed the
                                    "outside john."
But in my time
its fame was based on more descriptive terms
        like privy or the outhouse or chic sales
                    for reasons I have never learned.
An efficient simple structure, that's for sure
sort of hidden in the grove north of the house
        some thirty yards or more I'd say
        from where the sidewalk stopped.
A journey not so bad most of the time
                    unless it rained.
But hazardous in winter months
        with cold north winds and snow piled high.
Then I'd find all sorts of reasons to postpone
        the trip I knew eventually I'd have
                                    to take.
I'll not explain except to say
        it seemed a needless bit of pain.

The Farm

Our world then
      when I was growing up.
The house—two-story frame.
Base Camp One and hub of the wheel.
Center of the farmstead universe.
Starting place of all adventures.
Haven for a family together.
Guarded on four sides by woven wire fence and
                       unlocked gates.
Final destination of the driveway
      swinging in from the Jewell-Stanhope road
      then north past the red horse-barn
      and curving east between the crib and the
         scales to end at the turnabout—
           the house on the right
               the garage on the left.

And beyond all this—the farm.
Three hundred and twenty acres
stretching a mile along the Jewell-Stanhope road.
Starting at the Garden Center School
             a quarter-mile west
     and ending at Percy Wilson's place
            three-quarters mile east.
And all the land to the north
         for half a mile.
Four eighty-acre rectangles.
Each claiming its quarter-mile frontage.
Each admitting entry through a double gate.
Each encircled by rows of steel post sentinels
      holding waist-high bands of woven steel fence.
Each with its role to play
     in the lives of all of us.

That's the way it was in 1928—
      ten years after the world's Great War
      and a year before the Great Depression.
That's the way it was for a boy who's ten
            going on eleven.

The Family

There were seven of us then
when I was growing up
        believing as I did
        that all tomorrows were forever.

Seven of us.
My Mom and Dad, three brothers, counting me,
        one sister for the three of us,
        and then the hired man.

Seven of us.
To share the house and farm the land.
To talk at night
        about those things that families talk about—
        the price of corn, the newborn colt
        the miracle of Lindbergh's flight
                        to Paris all alone.

Seven human beings.
Laughing, talking, loving,
        fighting for our right to be.
So much alike in many ways.
And yet so different as all humans are
        in how we looked at things
        and how we dreamed our dreams.

His name was Benjamin
but everybody called him Ben
except the four of us who called him Dad.

Mom's name was Lillian
and some did call her that
but mostly she was Lilly to her friends
                or better yet just Lil.

Dad wasn't tall
perhaps five-nine or ten
        well built and strong
with brown hair flecked with grey
                and parted on the side.
His eyes a special shade of blue

expressing honesty and truth
with never anything to hide.

Mom was just as tall as Dad
    or taller by a shade perhaps.
Willowy slim when first they met I guess
but now with curves and softness
    all mothers ought to have.
Her eyes were walnut brown
with hints of deviltry and mischief
lurking in the corners when she laughed
    or when she told a tale she'd heard
                at Ladies Aid.

Perhaps Dad told us
    when we were young
about how come his right hand
only had two fingers and a thumb.
Perhaps we asked and if we did
as like as not he'd joke and have a little fun
    by telling how a bad witch took the other two—
        the index finger and the middle one.
And yet somehow we knew
about the accident one day when he was four
but big enough he thought
    to help the men put up the hay
and how his hand got caught
between the pulley and the door.
He claimed his hand as now designed
was better suited to the task
    of milking cows and scooping corn
        and pinching boys who wouldn't mind.

He had a way with horses, kids, stray dogs
        and white-faced Hereford steers.
They seemed to understand and trust
the outer gentleness and inner strength of his.

Mom had a way of pointing out the stars at night
    of soothing cares and calming fright
    of telling how a kitten's born
    and seeing beauty in a storm.

Dad's parents came from England
and Grandpa settled on the Iowa land
                    when he was young
before he married Mary Ann and built the house
where Dad and all us kids were born.

Mom's folks were German reared.
They started farming first in northern Illinois
then bought the farm when Mom was young
just two miles down the road from where
                    young Ben was growing up.

Being neighbors as they were
it wasn't strange they met
            and we were lucky that they did.

The first thing I knew
                    or can remember anyway
was there I was
sitting at the oilcloth-covered kitchen table
                        listening to the talk
and trying not to spill the milk.

I had been born of course
                    some time before
but didn't think about it then.
The third of four Read kids
now each assigned a table place
        along with Mom and Dad
                    and Lawrence the hired man.
Let's just say to set the picture straight
the year was nineteen twenty-eight.
If that was so, then I was ten.

Weldon sitting on my right
                    the oldest at fourteen
        could drive a team and own a gun
        and smoke corn silk behind the barn.
On certain days if I behaved
                I'd get to join the fun.
But mostly he just shooed me off
            and acted like I didn't belong.

Thirteen, blue-eyed and blond
      and just a year behind
Arline had learned in early age
      the art of winning women's rights.
She could, if dared, outrun, outclimb, outtalk
                most kids her age
and often did by first establishing the rules.
That's why she got to start in school
      the same year Weldon did.
It always seemed to work out right
      the two of them as pals.
He the stronger of the two.
She the more aggressive in a fight.

The youngest of the group was Bob.
He sat by Mom.
The visitors exclaimed
about the darling little boy of seven years
      with curly hair so blond
         and eyes so blue.
And all the while the rest of us complained
about how spoiled he was
and how he always got his wishes
      by trading wants for kisses.

He'd come up from Missouri
      early in the fall one year
a lanky blond young man
who combed his hair straight back
      and wore those high-bib overalls.
He said he'd like to hire out a month or two
         to help with husking corn.
So much a bushel, board and room
        until the work was done
      and then he'd head back home.
The standard way of doing things at harvest time.
He talked with Dad out in the yard
      fifteen minutes more or less.
Long enough at any rate for Dad
      to take the measure of the man.
And then the two shook hands

not knowing that this man named Lawrence
would stay for twenty-years—
        the seventh member of the family clan.
He drove a Model-T
and smoked Prince Albert in his pipe
                    or rolled his own
and taught us how to sing
                    "The Wabash Cannonball."

That's the way it was
        the seven of us then
waiting for each season to arrive
        reminding us again
        about how wonderful it was
        just to be alive.

Spring

Spring is so many things.
Soft whispered sounds of morning rain
                              disturbing sleep.
The nonsense talk of baby chicks.
The windmill asking to be free.

The Arrival

When did we first receive
        those first faint signals?
Where did they come from?
Signals hinting that spring was coming
even while winter was everywhere in command.

How did we get word?
Not from the calendar certainly
                although there was one
there on the wall by the telephone
sent by Horton Dick's hardware store
                and saying Merry Christmas.
Calendars tell only months and days and dates.
Not how one day will be so very special.

Word came, perhaps, in the early morning
        as we walked toward the barn.
In the quiet darkness
        the snow didn't creak under our overshoes
        the way it did the day before.

Or was it later on the way to the milk house
        with the first pails of warm milk?
From the half-light above
        came the faint call of wild geese
        traveling north.
Did we notice then the windmill fan
        high on the triangle tower of steel
        turning its face from north to south
        to receive the gentle caresses
                of a shy south breeze?

Could be imagining things now of course.
But there do seem to be buds on the end twigs
        of that big maple tree by the garage.
A little swelling anyway.

No definite promises yet.
Nothing to really pin hopes on.
But a suggestive whisper at least.

Encouragement enough to stay alert
        for other signals later in the week
                        or the week after that.

There could be little doubt now—
                not after yesterday anyway.
Assaulted by sun and south wind
        winter surrendered nearly all of its snow
        in the open spaces.
Only scattered pockets of resistance remain.
Grimy dirt-covered snow ridges
        hiding in the dark shadows of buildings
        waiting without hope
        for reinforcements that will never come.

Weeks earlier
        winter began its retreat to the north
        sneaking in only enough fresh snow troops
                        under cover of night
        to confuse small boys of its intentions.
Those troops quickly fading away
                before next day's noon
as advancing spring marched to final victory.

Now
with more love than malice
spring returns the snow of winter
to the air, the earth, and the streams and rivers
                from which it came.
And in a hundred ways
spring proclaims its victory
        and its seasonal occupation of the land.

An advance robin in the front yard
                head cocked to one side listening.
Waiting for a worm to make its first move.
Then, all at once, a yard full of robins.

A flock of blackbirds winging in from the south
        to check out the grove west of the barn.

A yellow-headed dandelion
        poking up through the brown grass
        pretending it had been there all the time.

The barn swallows returning
  to survey the scene from their perch
  along the lone telephone wire.

The fur-lined jacket hanging on the nail
     in the little kitchen.
No longer needed until winter returns.

Sparrows making quick flights.
Moving back and forth from nesting supplies
  to building sites under the barn eaves.

Talk now of field work
  of cleaning the cistern before spring rains
  of putting the sleds away, and the skates
  of taking the weather-stripping off the doors
  of garden plowing and kite flying
  and making slingshots
  and seeing the first ground squirrel.

Talk now of spring.

Baby Chicks

A rather ordinary day in March.
Not too cold and not too warm.
Just sort of in-between
                    but restless.
Quiet like but restless
        especially there inside the guard-house incubator
        now occupying bedroom space
        where weeks before a bed had been.

Inside those guard-house walls
inmates confined to eggshell prison cells
were growing stronger by the hour
        more cunning in their ways
        more sure their voices would be heard.

Then the breakout came
        starting first in early afternoon.
A wave of bold ones first
                    breaking free
        using pick-axe beaks to cut their cells
                    chanting liberty
        demanding entrance to the world
        and coaxing others to be brave.

By suppertime
successive waves of other freedom fighters
join the throng demanding food
        fresh water
        safe transport to the brooder house
                    underneath the mulberry tree.

Too late, too dark, too cold for that tonight.
A truce 'till morning then.
An interim agreement.
Temporary passage now
        to cardboard boxes placed behind the stove.
And then
        completion of the journey after breakfast.

Both sides agree.

The deal is closed.
A quiet murmur fills the room.
Our voices low.
All went as planned.
No need for them to know
      the whole affair was staged by Mom
          and set in motion weeks ago.

Even while the snow swirled down
Mom had the incubator brought inside
so she could make it ready
          for the drama we had seen.
She scrubbed it inside out with water boiling hot
          and laced with caustic lye and soap
and then she trimmed the burner wicks
          and filled the little tank with kerosene.
That done
she stage a two-day trial run
to make sure it would stay
      a steady ninety-eight degrees
      both night and day
before she trusted it with precious hatching eggs.

Three hundred fertile eggs that Mom had saved.
Three hundred fragile shells
      protecting lives within—
lives that couldn't start to be
until Mom placed them row on row
      on incubator hatching trays.
After that
for twenty days plus one
she turned each egg three times a day
      the way a feathered mother would have done.

The covered boxes quiet now behind the stove
except when Mom slips stragglers in
          still damp
disturbing those already there.
Brief muttered protests then.
Mom speaks some soothing words
      and quiet once again invades the room.

The morning transfer made without a hitch.
Mom did the planning in advance and double checked.
    Brooder house all clean and dry.
    Steady warmth at seventy-five.
    Chick hover raised up from the floor.
    Ground corn-cob litter spread out next.
    Feeders filled with tasty mash.

The brooder house.
Warm haven during days in March
        and into early April too.
A place to come in from the cold
to share the warmth
        and listen to the serenade of birds.
A place to let the bold ones come up close
      and peck the fingers of my hand.
A place to be alone.
A place to dream about the things I'd do
        when I grew up
but never really believing that I would
        nor sure I wanted to.

Orphan Lambs

There was always one it seemed.
At least one orphan lamb
given life on a bitter night
when winter tried for one last time
              to capture back its rights.
Always arriving after midnight—
there in the alleyway of the barn
         a maternity ward for twelve ewes
kept on the place for sentimental reasons
             as much as anything else.
Found in the morning at milking time.
Shivering there in cold and hunger
             still damp from birth.
Too weak to stand alone on spindle legs.
Rejected for unknown reasons.
Scorned by three mothers who gave birth
         during the night.
Six lambs in all.
Only five now claimed as kin.
The sixth unloved and unwanted—
        alone and vulnerable.
An orphan child ignored by one
who should have given warmth and food
             and loving care.

No time now to ponder parent-child relationships.
Little gained by placing blame
        on first that ewe and then another.
They have their reasons I suppose.
As good as those we give
        for thoughtless hurts that we impose.

Dry the newborn infant first
        with gunny sack and fresh clean straw
and give it warmth inside my fur-lined mackinaw.
Then hurry to the house.
Put it in the cardboard box
        half-filled with rags.

Place it then behind the stove
        the warmest place of all we know
        to start the process of adoption.

Mom finds a nursing bottle easily enough
                complete with rubber nipple.
I fill it halfway to the top
with fresh warm milk taken from the one
        who might have been the mother.
Standing now on wobbly legs
the famished newborn orphaned lamb
takes hold and gulps that milk with gratitude
concerned with content first of all
                        no matter the container.

And just as easily it seems
                with wagging tail
the lamb accepts the role bestowed by all
of pampered new child of the house
expecting any hour of the day
to have its wants attended to immediately.
How quickly, though, an infant orphan lamb
                in awkward adolescence
outgrows its place behind the stove
and needs a more appropriate abode
                for growing up a man.

Spring Seeding

Saturday figured to be the day
                        to start the seeding.
If it didn't rain before then anyway.
Seeding oats—the first field work of spring.
A two-man job.
A man and boy at any rate.
Man driving the team—
              boy keeping the seeder filled.
The north forty ready.
Everything else too.
Top box off the grain wagon
                      leaving two.
Whirlwind seeder cleaned and put in place.
Drive chain checked.
Weak links removed
              to run real smooth from wagon wheel
                          to seeder cogs.
Seed oats cleaned a month ago
              waiting now for transfer to the wagon box.

Cold Saturday but dry.
No rain in sight.
We'd start right after morning chores.
Two men, my Dad and me, first out
              with two-horse team and seed-filled wagon box.

The forty acres lie ahead.
Haunted now by barren death-grey stalks
              that yielded last year's crop of corn.
Stalks left standing through the winter months
              to catch the snow
              and keep the earth from blowing with the wind.
Waiting now in proud defiant rows
                      to guide the team,
they feel the biting sting of oats
              flung out against them
              by the whirling seeder fan.
The sound familiar.

Like winter's sleet
        against the windows of the house
            such a little time ago.

We pass.
The stalks still briefly stand
        before the final moment of surrender.
And then in wholesale execution
        chopped down, destroyed, returned to earth
        by round, revolving, knife-sharp blades
                            of tandem disk
        pulled by straining horses four abreast
        and driven by the hired man—
            a charioteer in overalls.

The tasks are done.
Old lives destroyed.
New ones begun.
The scattered seeds protected now
                    soil covered and serene
awaiting only rain and sun
to turn the field to green
before the golden harvest in the fall.

Corn Planting

Click—click—click—click
measured pulsing cadence
repeated beat of sameness
hypnotic rhythm of machine
coming from the distance of the field
more felt than heard
the source unseen
hidden for the moment beneath the rise
                              but known.

Click—click—click—click
machine and man and team of matching bays
sending messages of spring
along a half a mile of wire
        knotted for a purpose every forty inches
secured at either end to slender iron pegs
        thrust deep into the warming soil.

Click—click—click—click
I wait and watch and listen
        with coffee jug in hand
ready now to greet this man
who plants a straighter row of corn
than any other man around.

Click—click—click—click
a sharper sound
I see them now
stride—stride—stride—stride
heads bob—heads bob
click—stride—heads bob—click—stride
a perfect blend of horse and man
                in syncopated rhythm
the man astride his mount of calibrated steel
a box of corn on either side
fed down on call from planter wire
through tubes to furrows in the earth
and covered there by planter wheels.

Click—stride—heads bob—click—stride
kernels drop—three or four—each side
click—stride—heads bob
wheels turn—wheels cover—wire taut
click—stride—heads bob
team of bays—Dan and Pride—same size
click—stride—heads bob
matching steps—one to one
all day—all day
             until it's done.

Spring Farrowing

So much depends
on those selections made four months ago
of adolescent maidens of the lot.
Chosen gilts
picked to play the future prima donna roles
                    of motherhood in spring.

The script perfected through the years
calls for a cast of twenty-one
            plus one as understudy—maybe two.
Only one of five or six who might apply
will pass the rigid test imposed
by those who have the final say.
The others left to fatten in the lot
until their final destiny—
            a one-way trip to market later on.

Experience doesn't count of course
since none have played the role before.
All novices at giving birth
            and mothering the young.
But what about the families
of all these actresses-to-be?
We'll check that first and see
how many siblings each one had
and how the mother played her role
            in her appearance on the stage.
This one review enough
            to cut the field of applicants in half.

Screen next for size.
Not beauty and not grace
but size and thirftiness—
that pace of growth since birth
which separates the gainers
            from the losers in the lot.

One more question if you please
before the final vote is cast.
It must be asked.

How many nipples does each have
to serve as nursing stations for the young?
Each must have ten
        and twelve would almost guarantee
        selection for a starring role.

That's how it was the previous fall
when those selected maidens trim and fair
were singled out and taken from the feeding lot
to share a brief romance
        the suitor common to them all

then given special quarters to await
their curtain calls in farrowing stalls
as yet three months, three weeks, three days away.

And now this week and next at least
each has her turn at center stage.
Premier performers all
they act a drama some call miracle of birth
          and others simply label farrowing time.

Appropriately enough
the first
a white-robed gilt with spots of black
elects an after-midnight preview time
                              producing nine.
We'd hoped for ten but nine will do.
Five boys, four girls of average size
          soon dry and nursing well.
We'll save them all.

A double matinee is next.
The redhead giving birth to twelve.
The blond to only seven.
So two are taken from the one
          and given to the other—
related offspring after all
when we recall
each family has a common father.

In time the curtain falls.
The last performer takes her bows
          and steps from spotlight to the wings
to quickly change into her role of motherhood.

"How'd your gilts do, Ben,"
they'll ask my Dad next Saturday in town.
"Pretty good," he'll answer back.
"They averaged almost ten apiece,
          that's counting runts and all you know.
We'll lose a few I guess."
But all agree that's pretty good.

Morning Chores

It's different
doing morning chores in spring.
The routine's much the same as any other time
                but somehow not the same at all.

Different.
Starting with the time of getting up
and seeing light already there
                competing with the morning stars
until an hour later more or less
when Mom calls to the barn and says
that breakfast's almost ready to be served.

Light sneaking in my room to help me dress
        in cotton shirt and denim overalls.
No need to light the lamp.
It's almost out of kerosene in fact.

Different.
In the way I hurry past the kitchen range.
Its friendly warmth not needed now.
I use those minutes saved
to pause outside the kitchen door
and marvel at the wonders of it all.
The lingering morning mist
        there in the orchard to the east
reluctant now to take its leave
but knowing soon it must forsake
the fragrance of the apple blossoms pink.

The quietness of morning sounds
as though not sure the day's awake—
        not wanting to be rude.
Feet pushing into rubber boots.
The muted coos of mourning doves.
The gentle fluttering of wings
        as laying hens depart their roosts.
The plaintive plea from windmill fan
        asking for release to catch the morning breeze.
The whir of blackbirds taking leave
        from perches high atop the maple tree.

Such minutes wisely spent
diminish only briefly those still left
before the sun officially appears
to start its daily round
of helping earth and men.
No time to talk about the day.
No need to, actually.
We know the tasks that must be done
in sixty minutes that remain
and set about accordingly.

One boy
(as like as not it's me)
bareback astride a gallant steed
heads east across the plains
(the little pasture actually)
playing games of fantasy along the way.
One time a fearless warrior of the tribe.
The next a knight in full pursuit
of those who'd overthrow the Crown.
Or maybe just a cowboy of the West
rounding up a herd of thousands all alone
alert for bands of Indians
            lurking in the fields beyond.

All victories thus won
there but remains the simple chore
of bringing in the seven docile cows.
Spot, my pinto pony, white on red,
knew all along the purpose of our morning ride.
He never said a word.

One man or boy
(my brother probably)
starts his appointed rounds within the barn.
Horse mangers to the left filled first
with clover hay
tossed down from storage in the mow.
The grain box for each horse filled next
                seven ears of corn per share
carried in a basket from the crib.
The process then repeated on the right.

There seven stalls stand ready to receive
        the seven cows when they arrive.

In the alley of the crib
an empty three-tiered wagon waits.
It must be filled with corn
for after-breakfast feeding of the steers.
Another one the same in size
stands parked beneath the silo's loading shoot
braced firm to take a heap of sweet and sour feed
tossed down the shoot from thirty feet above.
Both tasks assigned the hired man.
He doesn't care for milking cows in any case.

It's understood by everyone
that only Dad can be in charge
of tending to the pampered gilts.
New mothers all
sharing with their young the same address—
house number one on Avenue de Swine.

I herd the cows into the barn
and let each find her place assigned
before I snap each stanchion shut
and take Spot to his stall and his reward
                for work well done.

The milking ritual begins.
A pleasant task in many ways
             at least in spring.
My throne a one-leg milking stool.
No thing of beauty to be sure
             but adequate enough.
The milk pail held between my knees
to catch the flow of milk
hand-squeezed from teats suspended from above
much like full fingers of a rubber glove.
A moment of contentment now
       lulled by the rhythm of the chore
and soothed by sounds familiar in the barn.
Horses nuzzling for grains of corn.
Sparrows taking sudden flight.

Pigeons making sounds of love.
Time to think if I'm alone
   of fantasies or things more real
and then to talk as others come to help
until the pails are full
and carried to the milk house
when the milking's done.

Although we didn't know it then
   or think about it anyway
the milk house represented change
from how things were before
   to how they were about to be.
A single step of progress some might say.
In earlier days
the pails of milk were left to cool
in caves beside the house
      or cellars underneath
where Nature surfaced thick rich cream
   for kitchen table or for sale.
The milk house soon became a modern place
where Nature's law and man's machines
   combined to do things differently.

There stands a metal robot five feet tall
    feet firmly bolted to the floor.
Its head's an empty bowl.
Two spouts for arms.
Its heart a pyramid of disks encased in steel.
The whole contraption thus designed to
    tear apart the milk.
For all its intricate design
the monster stands now motionless and mute
until some boy consents to twist its arm
and it becomes a whirling banshee thing
gulping milk poured in its top
before releasing its component parts—
cream for food and skim milk for the hogs.

The milk-house tank
   simple in design of corrugated steel

accepts its role as modern cooling place.
For a time it holds the ice-cold water
in its flow from windmill pump to outside tank
      where livestock quench their thirst
      and small boys sneak a naked dip
              on summer days.
The water cools a giant can of cream
      until its sale on Saturday
a gallon syrup pail of milk saved yesterday
           another saved today
a three-pound tin of butter
      churned Monday afternoon.

The whirling banshee stops its tune.
I look out through the milk-house door
and see the sun, impatient now,
nudge aside a fleecy cloud
      and take command of day.

The morning chores are done.

May Baskets

What casualness prevailed
among the four of us that night.
How feigned our innocence of date and day
although we'd spent the week before
preparing for the start of May.

No artist could have given greater care
designing offerings to share with spring.
Berry baskets
still with stains from last year's crop
the starting props for magic transformation
into wondrous works of art.
With help from Mom
they soon became lace-covered things
to hold some homemade fudge
or peanut brittle
or penny candy from the store
all hidden underneath the tissues white
                    and apple blossoms pink.

How obvious our excuses were
for staying in the house long after supper
accepting as we did all built-in risks
of being asked to dry the dishes
        or clean the chimneys of the lamps.
Nothing had been said at school.
A hint perhaps but nothing definite.
And yet somehow we knew
that we would be the first to hear the call
that made the waiting worth it all.

A growing tension now.
An urge suppressed to look outside
for signs of shadowy figures
seeking secret places they could hide—
        behind the barn, perhaps,
                or in the rafters of the crib.

A stealthy footstep on the porch.
We're sure we heard it.

Stillness for a moment more
and then the call rings out
      to shatter all illusions of surprise.
MAY BASKET
A mad dash out the door
           the four of us
in wild pursuit of neighbor kids
who must be found and tagged
           then brought to bay.
The last one found named king
with sacred right to pick the game we'd play
until the clock struck ten or later still
when by consent
we all agreed to end the day.

We knew we'd meet tomorrow night
      after supper if it didn't rain.
Then at some other place
new actors take the stage.
A new king crowned—a new game played.
Another night—another place
      until all nights of May have been erased.

Free Saturdays

Saturdays in spring sometimes were free
                       for boys at least
assuming certain IFs worked out appropriately.

IF nature honored our request
to send down rain on Friday night
        leaving fields too wet to cultivate.

IF someone didn't say in that event
it was the day to vaccinate the pigs
        or clean the laying house
        or fix the feedlot gate where it had bent.

IF extra hands weren't needed all the while
to cut the yellow thistles
        or put new shoes on Dan and Pride
        or dig the ditch for laying tile.

IF nothing else stood in the way
the day was ours—our freedom won
        right after morning chores were done.

So it was some Saturdays in spring
that I was free to pick the escapade
from all the previous plans I'd made.
Perhaps I'd go alone
stalking mighty tigers of the land
armed only with a trusty bow I'd made by hand.
Or would a slingshot be a better weapon
                  for my prey?
In a way more difficult to make
but with a greater accuracy at fifty feet.
I'll use a Y-branch from a youthful oak
        to form the grip.
To that I'll tie two narrow rubber strips
        cut from an inner tube.
The leather tongue from some discarded shoe
will do just fine for missile pouch.
A boy of nine
        with such a piece of weaponry

58

could fling a smooth round stone a mile—
                 well, fifty yards at least.

If hunting tigers seemed too tame a way
to spend a Saturday that's free
then there were other games to play.
The grove of maples, oaks, and stately elms
could turn into a jungle lair for Tarzan
and his mighty band of barefoot men
        all dressed in tattered overalls.
We'd make breath-taking sweeps
                 from tree to tree
on jungle vines disguised so cleverly
as hay ropes borrowed from the barn.
No harm could come from that I think.

I knew of course there was a chance that
fickle Nature would forget to stop the rain
leaving Saturday as dripping wet
        as Friday night was meant to be.
But freedom in the rain was freedom anyway
no matter that we'd have to stay inside the barn.

The hayloft almost empty now the perfect place
for famous circus acrobats to do their thing.

The trumpets sound.
There is a hush among the thousands gathered there.
The roll of drums.
And high above the multitude a fearless lad
grabs hold the slender strand
casts off and swings far down
to zoom aloft again
and then to drop unharmed
onto the pile of musty hay that still remains.
The audience bursts forth with wild applause.
The curtain falls.

Dad calls and says it's time for chores.
Another Saturday of freedom ends.

The Kite Flyer

Saturdays in spring were sometimes free
                              for doing many things
but mostly they were free for flying kites.

There was no way—no way at all
to make believe I didn't understand
the meaning of the challenge when it came
on orders from the hawk
                              delivered by the wind.
The bird in flight looked down as if to say,
"No barefoot boy could build a kite
to fly as high as I, a lonely hawk, can fly."
I knew the truth of that.
And yet there was no choice.
I had to try.

Nature fashioned hawks to fly that's true.
But could she in her wisdom have designed
another bird more beautiful or proud
than this one now so recently created
                              by a country boy of nine?
Its cross-stick ribs cut from a lath
                              straight-grained and true
then sanded smooth.
Its spreading wings of white
once butcher paper from the store.
Its tail a long thin colored strip of rags
borrowed from the sewing basket in the hall.

Poised now and proud.
A boy-made hunting falcon eager to be free
                              to ride the wind
and meet the challenge from the mighty hawk
        still claiming rights to all the sky.

A maiden testing flight at first
                              some fifty feet or so
to check design against the wind
and plan the final strategy.

This done
the bird is tossed aloft.
It climbs on outstretched paper wings
        to meet its destiny above—
its lifeline to the earth below
a fast unwinding length of string
            held by the boy.

He looks up in the sky and envies both
the kite he's made
            and mighty soaring hawk
who knowing that he's won the game
            now flies away.

Cultivating Corn

The corn's up.
A simple statement certainly—three words.
Enough in any case
        to stop all other talk at supper time.
You sure?
Yup. I checked this afternoon.
Can't make out the rows as yet
        but it's coming through for sure—
                no doubt of that.

What about the stand?
Looks good.
At least what's up so far.

The eighty farthest from the house
first planted on the fifth of May
now ten days later giving life
to a million shoots of corn or more
light green and tender
coming through the crust of earth
                seeking sun.
Eight hundred hills of three shoots each
and sometimes four
spaced forty inches in the row for half a mile.
Four hundred rows
to fill the half a mile of width
same forty inches separating rows.

If the weather keeps its warmth
for five days more
the field will stand for dress parade
as inch-tall sentinels of green
form row on row for all to see.
In ten days more
this wide expanse of green
will turn into a battlefield.
Men and boys on steel machines
will venture forth to wage a six weeks' war
against marauding hordes of weeds
                now massing for attack.

Two weeks at most from now
but time enough to check and overhaul
four two-wheeled chariots of death
that we—two men, two boys—
                will ride into the fray.

The cultivator.
So simple its design
            so innocent its name
            and yet so deadly in its violent acts—
so true of any war machine I guess.
Pulled by a team of bays or blacks
its gaunt steel wheels precisely spaced
straddle but a single row
and on each side suspended from a beam
hang three sharp guillotines
arrayed to catch and execute
                the guilty weeds.

Let's go.
A week before the end of May
the waiting's done.
Two men, two boys in denim uniforms
and helmets made of straw
guide their machines into the field.
The battle has begun.

Each stakes a claim—
a hundred rows
one quarter of the field
twenty acres of terrain to clear
                of enemies of corn.

Excitement now.
The horses move out on command.
The flashing killer blades knife down
destroying all who dare invade the land
                between the sacred rows.
A first sweep to the north.
Then back again.
The horses turn.
Another round and then the next

and still another after that
until the truce at noon.

And so the battle will be fought
each morning and each afternoon
for forty days or more—
at least from now until the end of June.

Making Hay

One third in blossom as it is
the clover field can't wait much longer
                              for its turn.
Haying has to start on Monday next.
A welcome break from cultivating corn.

Hold back the rain a week.
Bring on the sun.
Sprinkle sky with friendly clouds
        and let the sequence of events
        produce four towering stacks of hay
                        rectangular and trim
        with rounded tops to shed the rain.

Monday finally comes.
The mower moves out first at nine.
Its innards oiled.
Its five-foot cutter bar concealing
        guarded shark-teeth sickle knives
                freshly sharpened on the stone.

A final check.
All morning dew is gone.
The sickle reaches out along the ground.
The gears engage.
The horses feel the subtle slap of reins
                        and move.
In whispered protest
        a five-foot swath of clover gently falls
                        behind the slashing blade.
By noon a hundred fragrant swaths and more
                        lie wilting in the sun.
Enough for now.

The windrow rake
        a strange machine of awkward grace
now takes the place of mower in the field.
Crablike
it moves astride the fallen swaths
and lets its slender fingers made of steel

reach down to gently lift the fallen hay
and sweep it into endless rows
                    for curing through the night.

The second day.
The buckrake and the stacker
stand waiting in the morning sun.
The two of them
          so different in design
          so odd in shape and size
and yet so cleverly contrived
to help men gather in the hay
                    and make the stack.

Pulled by a team of bays hitched wide apart
          and driven by the hired man
the buckrake slips its six-foot fingers
underneath a row of hay and piles it back.
Its paunch is full.
It pulls away
and takes its load to where the stacker stands
                    chained to the earth
much like a catapult of old.

The rugged giant waits.
Its arms at rest on either side
          support a single ten-foot hand
          with slender wooden fingers
          reaching out along the ground
          ready to receive the offering of hay
          when brought by buckrake from the row.
Then on command
it lifts the load above its head
and flings it back upon the stack
                    the men now build.

The day unfolds.
The sky is clear.
The sun is warm upon our backs.
We're making hay.

First Flight

I'd find them there
huddled in a corner of the loft
                untended to and cold
and easy prey for cats who happened by.
Perhaps they'd fallen from their nests
        high in the rafters of the barn
or tried too soon to test their wings in flight.

I never knew.
It didn't really matter after all.
The mission now was clear—
to turn these half-grown pigeons into pets
with corn and drink and tender loving care.

A box half-filled with straw
and placed behind the kitchen stove
would serve as home for now at least.
No problem there.
They couldn't fly in any case.
Too young as well to eat alone
        no matter what the fare.
And so a technique improvised
by holding wide the beak to force-feed corn
until the youngsters learned the knack
        of eating on their own.
The smoke house empty of its meat
        more private than the house
could now become the second home
for growing birds—half-tame, half-wild
and keen to fly and break their bonds with earth.

Clean first with scalding water
                laced with lye.
Replace the solid door with screen
and build a roosting place above the floor
                fresh carpeted with straw.

Bring in the fledgling pilots next
and give them half a day at least
to get accustomed to the place

67

before I teach them how to fly
so they can later race the wind.

Short flights at first.
A gentle toss from where I stand
to safety of the roost three feet away—
                    no more than that.
Hold them if they fall to calm their fears.
Then toss again
        until they've got the hang of it.
After that a feast of corn picked from my hand—
                    a just reward for doing good.

Another lesson in the afternoon.
A third when supper's done.
More distance now.
A quiet talk when darkness comes
to tell them why a boy like me
                needs birds for friends.

Progress through the week suggests
that training for the solo flights can start
as soon as chores are done on Saturday.
Hunger is the motivating force.
This means, of course, no feast of corn
the Friday night before the scheduled flight.
I hope my friends will understand when
                    morning comes.
I think they will.

The lessons now begin.
A short hop first from roost to hand
            to take the offering of corn.
Then back to roost to try again.
Each flight a little longer than before
until there's confidence
to go the distance of the house without a miss.

Two days go by
before the shift outside the house
to taste the cherished fruits of flying free
            in company of wind and sky.

A time for testing strength of wings
     for soaring high
          for sweeping low.

Their lessons learned
they fly away.
A small boy stands below with corn in hand
and love
and waits for their return.

Barefoot Day

How come I wonder
they never mark Barefoot Day on the calendar.
Easter is there
        sometime after Washington's birthday.
And Memorial Day and Fourth of July.
Those days are there
marked plain as anything on the
calendar from Horton Dick's hardware store
        hanging on the wall by the telephone.
But never a date marked Barefoot Day
        the most important date of all
                when spring came anyway.

There was no way I guess
for mothers and sons to quite agree
on what that date should be—
sons thinking it should come
        the first warm day in March
or April when the snow had gone away
and mothers holding out for late in June
                or even early in July.

Without a calendar to set us straight
there always was a big debate like this:
Can I go barefoot, Mom?
No, it's too (cold), (early), (late), (wet).
I'll stay right in the yard for just a little while.
No, you'll step on a nail.
I'll be careful.
No, if you step on a rusty nail
                you'll get lockjaw and die.
Ronald's mother let him go barefoot yesterday.
I'm not Ronald's mother.
Please.
Well, for ten minutes if you're careful.

Mom (a plaintive wail).
What happened?
I stepped on a rusty nail.

I told you to be careful.
Will I get lockjaw and die?
Of course not silly boy.
Who ever heard of a little boy getting lockjaw?
No need to cry and make a scene.
I'll clean it out with kerosene.
That hurts.
Of course it does.
Can I go out tomorrow please?

Spring House-Cleaning

It would come sometime in May.
I'd say about a week or so
    after Dad had taken down the heating stove
    and stored it straightaway out in the shed.
Some day in any case
    between corn-planting time
    and putting up the hay.

At breakfast Mom would say real loud,
"I plan to clean this dirty house
    and I plan to start today."
A factual statement obviously.
But more than that.
Her words contained a warning and a threat.

So little time to seek and find
those precious treasures
    hoarded through the year
lest they be classified as trash
    and tossed aside or burned.
What tragedy.

The broken kite and bits of string.
The corn-cob pipe.
The rabbit fur and leather straps.
Gopher traps that never worked.
The Wild West pistol made of pine.
A piece of canvas tinged with mold.
That length of twine.
Stones with flecks I knew were gold.

The race to find those treasures rare
and take them to the barn
    for hiding in another secret place.

All hands stand ready now
    to man the battle stations.
Mom's in command.
Roll up the parlor rug
and take it out
    for beating on the line.

With care
dismantle kitchen stovepipes next
                      steady as you go.
Keep that soot from spilling forth
until you have them out of doors
                for cleaning and repair.
Transport and store beneath the sky
all furniture and bric-a-brac
             from downstairs rooms.
Leave only naked floors
          for cleaning in the afternoon
          before the coating with shellac.
Wash windows
mend the screens
and scrub the porch as well.
When that is done
repair the handle on the pump
          and fix the outside cellar door.
With luck we'll finish everything
before the start of evening chores.

Excitement mounts.
Anticipation of adventures and rewards.
The kitchen stove is down
          the floors shellacked.
No trespassing is allowed
          in any of the rooms.
We'll eat in town at Chuck's Cafe.
We'll stay outside when we get home
          and talk long after dark
and after that we'll build a narrow walk
from kitchen door to stairway leading up above.
Like stealthy pirates of another day
we'll walk the planks
with only lighted lamps to show the way.

Spring Is So Many Things

Spring is so many things.
The scent of lilacs in the yard
      and newborn puppies underneath the barn.
The dust of clover hay tossed down
      and blossoms of the apple trees.
The breath of horses being fed their hay
      and damp earth freshly plowed.

Soft whispered sounds of morning rain
             disturbing sleep.
The nonsense talk of baby chicks.
The windmill asking to be free.
The sparrows taking early leave.
The distant thunder faintly heard.
The creaking gate when first disturbed.
Contented whispers in the night
      as breeze and leaves discuss
         their right to be.

Grey morning mist against a multi-colored sky.
Sparkling dew held for display
      by shy and slender blades of grass.
Pink cherry blossoms taking bows.
A cotton ceiling fashioned by the clouds.

The touch of rain.
The feel of leather gloves.
The softness of a kitten being held.

Spring is so many things.

Summer

Don't let it rain tomorrow, Lord.
Don't let it rain on my parade.
Don't let it rain tomorrow, please,
not after all the plans I've made
           to celebrate the Fourth.

Summertime

Summertime.
Coolness of early morning.
Dew soaking my shoes
     as I drive the cows in from pasture.
Stillness at noon.
Men and animals
     seeking shade and respite from the sun.
Soft laughter at night.
Far-off flashes of lightning
     raising the curtain on a summer storm.

Summertime.
Dragonflies skimming the little pond
     as it pleads for new life from fresh rain.
White lather on straining horses
     hitched four abreast pulling the binder.
Green moss fouling the water of the stock tank
     now that the cattle are sold.

Summertime.
Thirst-quenching cool water from a gallon jug
wrapped in a wet gunny sack
     and left in cool shade of tall weeds.
Sharp tang of forbidden green apples
taken from the special tree in the orchard
     on my way to the garden to hoe weeds.
Sweet juicy taste of ripe watermelons
borrowed from Cliff Taylor's melon patch
     after catching crawdaddies
          in the drainage ditch.

Summertime.
The excitement of wondering
     how many stars there really are
          and what lies beyond
     how caterpillars turn into butterflies
          and what happens after that
     how a swallow knows the best way
          to build a mud nest in the barn

how a hawk can fly so high for so long
without getting tired.

Day sounds.
Creaking cultivators making last assaults
on weeds invading knee-high corn.
Sickle knives on the oat binder
slicing through ripe yellow oat stems.
Horses stomping on dry ground
to shake away biting flies.
Mothers calling young sons in hiding
to avoid chores mothers remember.

Night sounds.
Crickets and locusts tuning up for their
night-long concert.
A lonely Model-T driving down the gravel road
and back again two hours later.
The barking of a neighbor's dog far off
and I wonder why.
The wind sighing in the mulberry tree
before the rain.
The thunder of my heartbeat
as I lie looking at the stars
wondering what it would be like to die.
Summertime.

Harvest

The field of oats is ready.
A sea of amber stems
      with waves of golden grain.
This ripened fruit of seeding in the spring
      lies ready now for harvesting—
      a product of the earth and gentle rain
          and summer sun.
It stretches east a quarter-mile
      and north for twice as far.

Ready now and vulnerable.
Strangely restless in submission.
It sees the morning sun retrieve the dew
and hears the south breeze brushing by
      whispering that men will come today
        to start the harvesting.

The binder first with Dad in charge
and then the three of us to build the shocks
      protection from the rain
      until the threshing starts.

We'd worked the day before to set the stage.
The binder taken from the shed.
Its innards cleaned and freshly oiled.
New balls of binder twine inserted in the box
      and threaded through those metal fingers
      that somehow tie a perfect knot.
The platform canvas checked for broken slats.
The same for those that catch the falling grain
      for transport to the platform on the side.
There other mechanisms take command
      to form and tie a bundle on the spot.
Thus bound and tied
the bundle falls onto the carrier below
until it's joined by three or four
to drop row after row
      around the eighty-acre plot.

There's nothing now that need delay the start.
The sun has swept the field of dew.
Four horses hitched abreast stand waiting patiently.
A final check.
Then from his iron seat above
          Dad gathers in the reins and says Giddap.
We stand and watch.
The horses step ahead as one.
The binder moves astride its power wheel of steel.
The giant reel now slowly turns
and nudges standing stems
          to meet the slashing sickle bar.
They fall in silent stricken swaths
upon the moving canvas belt
until they're gathered, tied, and dropped—
          tethered groups in bundles now
          no longer free to greet the sun
               or feel the cooling rain.

A hundred yards or so the outfit moves.
Then Dad says Whoa.
The horses stop.
Silence reigns as checks are made.
A look for signs that everything is working well—
          the sickle bar, the canvas belts
          the tension spring that tells the tripping rod
               how big the bundles ought to be.

"She looks okay you think?" Dad asks.
"She's running smooth," we say.
"No problems we can see."
That said
Dad mounts his iron seat again
          and gives his bamboo pole a flick.
The horses know without a word
they can begin their journey 'round the field.

We three
          my brother and the hired man and me
wait 'till the binder's made a second round
before we start to build the shocks
from bundles dropped along the ground.

80

It's ten o'clock.
We walk to different places in the field
                              to work alone.
The rhythm of the task returns in time.
I stoop and take two bundles by their twine
and in a single motion swing them up
to let them fall with heads entwined
                    to stand together as a pair.
I stoop again and take two more
              to flank the two now standing there.
Two more again to flank the other end
              and make an overlapping row of six.
Now one on either side for eight.
A final stoop to lift and spread apart
              a single bundle for the cap.
Other bundles lie serene on stubble top.
I play the scene again.
I know that I can build a shock
that looks as neat and stands as well
              as any fashioned by the hired man.

The sky is clear.
The sun is hot.
My cotton shirt is soaking wet with sweat.
And yet my pride won't let me stop—
              not for another hour anyway.
The binder comes around
and Dad hands down the water jug
                    to let me quench my thirst.
"You're working pretty hard," he says.
"I'm fine."
"You ought to take a little rest you know
                              from time to time."
"Okay."
He waits a minute more
to let the horses catch their breath
but just as much to let me know
he thinks I'm doing fine
and that's enough to last me through the day.

A boy can be a man at harvest time.

Threshers

Let's say they finished up at Taylors
        late on Tuesday afternoon.
So in the sequence of the threshing ring
                our place was next.
Just as we'd be doing chores
we'd hear the tractor pull the rig into our drive
          and leave it there beside the barn.

A magic monster of a thing
          the thresher was.
It stood on massive iron wheels
with gaping mouth held ten feet from the ground.
A mouth with canvas tongue and metal fins
      designed to gobble up oat bundles
      about as fast as two men threw them in.
Its giant shell of steel
concealed all kinds and shapes of things
that whirred and hummed and shook
until the oats were parted from the straw
and poured forth from the spout
         that swung out from its side.
The straw became the victim of a wind so fierce
it made you think a hurricane had come
to blow it through a twelve-inch tunnel pipe
      snaking out and upward from the end
      and moving slowly left to right
          and back again.

We're up before the sun on threshing day.
We've got to get the chores out of the way
         and breakfast done
before Perc Wilson comes at six
to fix a broken belt or two
      and get things ready for the start.
The tractor's his.
By everyone's consent he runs the rig.
It's owned by all the neighbors in the ring
      who pay so much a day for tractor rent.

First off
they pull the thresher to the lot
and place it on the spot Dad wants the stack.
It's lined up so the wind
will carry dust and dirt away
from all the working men.

It takes at least sixteen to do the threshing job.
Ten men with each a team and rack
to load and haul the bundles from the field
        and feed them to the big machine.
One man to handle two tight wagons
needed for the transfer of the grain
        from thresher to the storage bins.
Two men to scoop the grain when it arrives.
Two more to stack the straw.
The final one who runs the rig
and stands atop its quivering back
        to make sure everything is working right.

The most important jobs I guess
were delegated to the boys who were about.
How else would water jugs get filled
        or needed wrenches gotten from the shed
        or oil cans fetched
        or gates kept closed
        or messages of great import
                get carried back and forth?

From time to time if I were asked
I'd get to take a turn
at pitching bundles from the rack.
Or maybe there was need for extra hands
to tend the wagons as they filled with grain
        and drive them to the bins and back again.
If everything worked out
I got to claim the right
to help Perc Wilson run the rig.
This meant I climbed atop the monstrous thing
and stood with hands behind my back
                feet wide apart
to be a big shot for a while.

At threshing time
    Mom worked as hard as anyone.
She'd start to run
the minute she got breakfast dishes done.
Right now I don't recall
the actual sequence of events
that started shortly after six
    and ran through dinner call at noon.
But here's about the way it was.

Put all leaves in dining table
    stretching it from wall to wall.
Set places for at least ten men
    or maybe even twelve.
Peel apples from the pail and slice
and mix with sugar, cinnamon and spice
    to make five apple pies.
Baste a haunch of dark red beef
    and pot roast in the oven.
Pick green beans and beets with tops
    for cooking fresh in iron pots.
Select three heads of cabbage at the time
    for shredding fine and making slaw.
Bring potatoes from the cellar
    to peel and boil for mashing later.
Make a washroom for the men
with pails of water left to warm
    and fresh towels hung on nails.

It took three days at least
to get the threshing done—
long days of plain hard work
but days of fellowship and fun.

I always felt a little sad
the day the threshing rig pulled out.

Cattle Drive

Dad always made arrangements
                early in the week.
He'd order railroad cars
         and book the wooden holding pens
                    he'd need.
He'd tell the local agent of the line
about the hundred head of steers
         that he'd be shipping Saturday night.
That way they'd reach Chicago just in time
                for Monday's market trade.

That done
the news would spread about
that Ben was shipping out on Saturday.
Other men with corn-fed steers at home
would wonder now if they should do the same.
Feeding cattle was a gambling game at best.

Every summer farmers had to guess
about the market trend for fattened steers.
Sell right now and get the offered rate
       or wait a little longer on the bet
        that prices might go higher later on.
Each year in early fall
Dad bought a hundred white-faced yearling steers
       from ranchers in the west
        and brought them home to fatten in the lot.
They'd go on pasture first
       and make a little gain.
Then for a while
they'd have the run of cornfields
         after harvesting was done.
But just as soon as winter came
they'd go into the lot and start to put away
       twice daily feeds of silage, corn, and clover hay.
The payoff, if there was one, came in June
           or early in July
about the time we finished laying by the corn.
Sometime in there Dad set his mind

and then he'd say at suppertime
"I guess we'll ship the steers next week."
And that was that.

To tell the truth
I never gave much thought
to how much profit there might be
                    or how much loss
for all the corn and all the months of work
that went into the feeding of those steers.
Not until much later in my years
did I appreciate the hopes and fears
that Mom and Dad kept hidden from us kids.

For now it was enough to know
that we'd be shipping out next Saturday.
Enough excitement in that day alone
to last a boy a month or so because
                    here's how it was.

We're up before the sun announces day
to get the milking done
and give the steers a final feed
before we turned them out at dawn
to start the final drive to town
                    four miles away.

The work assignments settled in advance
but not without some argument at first
about which boy could claim the right
to saddle up and ride our pinto pony, Spot,
and who would have to take the sorrel mare—
                    a sorry second choice.
As like as not we ended up by drawing straws.

In any case regardless of the draw
I got to play the daring role of cowboy for a day
as trail boss for a dozen hands or more—
                    in fantasy at least.
I had the awesome task
of making sure this thundering herd of mine
        stretching out for miles along the trail
would make it through Apache land

until we'd meet up with the railroad line
somewhere out in Kansas.

It wasn't quite like that of course
seeing as we only had a hundred head all told.
Even so they scattered pretty hard
the minute we released them from the yard.
Then it took some expert riding on our part
to round them up and get them moving down the road.

After that
we'd have a fairly easy go for quite a while.
The hired man would lead the way.
Dad walked behind.
The two of us on horseback did patrol.
We'd ride ahead and guard the gates
that led into the neighbors' fields
or move along the ditches of the road
to prod the lagging ones ahead.

By eight o'clock or so
we'd reach the edge of town
and those fat steers would spook real good.
It might have been the feel of pavement underfoot
or just that people lined Main Street
to see Ben's cattle moving through.

Oh, actually,
there only were a few that acted up.
And I was always proud for the excuse
to race my steed before the watching crowd
as though the whole herd might stampede
and wreck this little town.

They never did.

It didn't take too long
before we had them headed through the gate
into the stockyard's holding pens.
Once there they'd rest and eat and wait
until four-thirty in the afternoon
and then we'd load them on the train
to take their final journey to Chicago.

I'd take one final gallop through the town
and head for home
wishing I had been alive
to help with cattle drives in olden times.

Fourth of July

Don't let it rain tomorrow, Lord.
Don't let it rain on such a special day.
Don't let it rain so Dad will have to say,
"We might as well stay home, kids,
      it's too wet out for ducks to fly."
Don't let it rain, Lord.
Not tomorrow.
Not on the Fourth day of July.

I never really thought the Lord had time
to pay attention to such pleas as that
especially when I only made them in my mind
                and not out loud.
But then it never hurt to try.

I guess a boy starts planning for the Fourth
      sometime around the first of May.
At least I always did.
That gave me two months anyway
to build my hoard of hand-earned cash
kept secret in an empty baking-powder can
I stashed away beneath the porch.

Some of the earnings came from Mom
for doing special chores around the house
like beating rugs
      or washing down the kitchen walls.
Some came from Dad.
An extra dime or two from time to time
      for working extra hard
or pennies he might find
      in pockets of his overalls.
And then Aunt Babe with no boys of her own
would often phone up Mom
and ask if one of us three boys might find
the time to help her with some tasks she had.
When that call came
I always made a special point
      of being most available of all.

No wage was ever mentioned in advance
but I could take a chance on getting paid
ten cents an hour anyway
            and sometimes more than that.

One day
            along about the end of June I guess
I'd sneak the baking-powder can up to my room
and make a final count of all I'd earned.
I'd spread the precious contents on the bed
and make a guess of total worth
            before the final adding up began.
By guessing lower than the fact
I could extract an added bit of pleasure
                        from the act.
I guess I still do that.

If it had been a really prosperous year
the bed-top count might show as much as say
            three dollars fifty cents
            or some such glorious amount.
Enough in any case
to make me tingle with anticipation
            of all the choices to be made.

Regardless of the final mark the total reached
at least a dollar must be set aside and saved
for spending at the celebration in the park.

This year I knew without a doubt
the man who said for just a dime
he'd guess my weight within ten pounds
would go down in defeat
            and I would win the Kewpie doll.

Having practiced throwing rocks at cans
            all summer long
I had strong confidence regardless of my size
that I could knock those bottles off the shelf
            and win myself another fancy prize.

Hamburgers cost a dime and pop five cents
and cotton candy ten cents more
                        for twenty-five all told.

So all in all it wasn't very wise
not to save a dollar s worth of change
for spending on the Fourth.

I took that dollar out
but then I had to face the awesome task
of knowing how to allocate the hard-earned cash
                    that still remained.
The big decision first.
Firecrackers got to claim
at least three-quarters of the final sum.
They returned more fun per nickel spent.
What was left would have to be enough
        to buy some sparklers
        a Roman candle—maybe two
        and other stuff like that.

The firecracker choices ranged
from buying lots of tiny ladyfingers
        that only gave out little pops
to buying giant cherry bombs that cost five cents
but blew the top right off a two-pound coffee can.
Other choices ranged between those two extremes.
And long before I had the dismal luck
to hear our military planners use the phrase
I tried to allocate my funds in such a way
        that I would get most bang per buck.

I knew the others hoped it wouldn't rain.
Mom said she had her face all set to celebrate.
Even though Dad didn't rate the day so high
                as all of us did then
I knew he'd like to watch the baseball game
        and talk with all the other men
        about those things men talk about.

Here's how it was the morning of the Fourth
                if no rain came.
We'd hurry through the chores so fast
                you wouldn't believe.
Then one of us would take the chicken-catcher out
        to snare two broilers by their legs
        and ring their necks right off.

Mom scalded them and picked them clean
while sitting on the giant rock
                    out by the big elm tree.
The only time that rock was ever used
                    as far as I could see.
She'd fry the chickens in a pan
            and fix the salad in a bowl
            and bake two cherry pies
and do the other things that must be done
to feed a hungry crew of six that afternoon.

While that was going on
us boys would take a bunch of firecrackers out
and do some pretty crazy things we thought were fun.

We'd put a two-inch cracker in a jar
to see how far the broken glass would fly.

We'd hold a cherry bomb and light it in our hand
and let the fuse about explode the thing
before we tossed it in the air and ran.

Sometime after ten
we'd get the call from Mom.
"You boys come in and get cleaned up
                    before we go to town."

Don't let it rain tomorrow, Lord.
Don't let it rain on my parade.
Don't let it rain tomorrow, please,
not after all the plans I've made
                    to celebrate the Fourth.

Summer Illusions

I climb down from the ledge and pause
                    naked and alone
anticipating stillness
        listening to quiet sounds
                watching deep still water
                    scorn the sun.

An Arab sheik
my trek across a hundred miles of burning sand
        ended now
        at this oasis in the desert land.

A fearless Indian brave
sent forth so many moons ago
in search of ancient tribal lands once lost
now found again at last
        around this hidden mountain lake.

The sole survivor
of the tragedy at sea that took all other lives
                    sparing me.
Drifting aimlessly for weeks.
Now saved.

This tiny island with its emerald lagoon awaits.
The stillness of my lonely world
now broken by a stealthy step above.
I turn.
From up above Ron Wilson's voice comes down.
"You goin' swimming?"
"Yeah."
"I thought your mother said you couldn't go."
"She said I could today I think."

I dive into the waiting sea.
No matter that illusions wash away.
A gravel pit two miles from home
is still a magic place to be on Saturdays.

Dam Builders

We'd done the secret engineering survey
               late in spring.
We'd picked the spot and made a pact.
We'd build a giant earth-filled dam
across the raging stream
      right after harvest in July.

Once built with stones and clay
      and branches from the willow tree
we'd have a perfect summer place
to swim and fish or lie along the shore
and watch a waterfall spin rainbows in the sky.
We dreamed of how a lake would stretch upstream
about as far as you could see
and be so wide
you'd need a boat to get from side to side.

We met at Wilsons
the day the work was scheduled to begin—
        the four of us
    my brother and the Wilson boys and me.
We loaded all our building gear
onto a two-wheeled cart
and hauled it to the spot we'd picked before
      being careful not to let the neighbors see.

First off
we slowed the water's flow by laying rocks
     big as a loaf of bread I guess
         across the riverbed.
Then we drove sharp willow stakes down deep
          on either side
     to keep the rocks in place.
We laced the stakes with cattail reeds and
sunflower stalks and giant weeds of every kind
      to form a double water-shield.
Once that structure was in place
we raced against the rising tide
to add more giant stones.

We filled the gaps between
with matted grass and sticky clay
to seal the cracks where water trickled through.

We must have used a ton of stuff
and when the gosh-darned thing was done
we were so wearied out
we couldn't have the fun we'd dreamed about.
But there'd be other days
            or so we thought
when we could reap the sweet rewards
from all our sweat and toil.

It didn't work that way.
I'll tell you why
            even though it spoils the tale.

The locale of our engineering dam
was really not the raging stream
I mentioned at the start.
In actual fact
it was the steep-banked drainage ditch
            no more than four feet wide
that started west of Garden Center School
and snaked on east for several miles
accepting run-off water from the tiles
that drained the neighbors' fields.

The dam we built so expertly
was what a well-built dam should be
            and did just what it was supposed to do.
It stopped the flow of water in its tracks
and backed it up for quite a ways
to make what could have been at least
            an honest swimming place
if not the kind of lake we told about before.

The problem was
the backed-up water also blocked the outlet tiles
and when it rained that night
the run-off water had no place to go
except to form a different kind of lake
where no lake ought to be—
            right there in neighbor Taylor's field.

It didn't take us long to figure out
that we were in a serious jam
when neighbor Taylor happened by to chat with Dad
                right after Sunday morning chores.
We knew their conversation in the yard
just had to be about that dam we'd built.
It was.

When Dad came in the house
he didn't say a word for quite a while.
He sort of smiled
        and drank the coffee Mom had poured
as though he knew what he was like
when he was growing up a boy.
When we were worked up to a fever pitch
he turned to Mom and told her
                in an offhand sort of way

that beavers
        never seen around these parts before
had evidently been at work
building dams in neighbor Taylor's drainage ditch.
He said that while he couldn't tell for sure
these might be beavers of a special kind
        having two legs rather than the normal four.
In any case he said
it was the nature of the beasts
to go away for good
if someone just could find the time
to tear apart their dam
                and let the water through.

With such an observation made
he turned to us real serious like
and asked if we would care to tackle such a task
instead of doing what we'd normally do
                on summer Sunday afternoons.
It didn't take us long to answer yes
and get outdoors in record time
        to finish up the chores.
We wondered all the while how come it was
that boys could get themselves in such a mess.

Even though the Wilson boys came out to help
we didn't think the tearing down this time
was quite the fun the building up had been.

Knowing Dad
I'd say he had that very thought in mind.

Saturday Night in Town

Mom calls through the screen door.
A warning.
"Supper's ready in ten minutes."
I stand naked in the wash house.
My bath almost finished.
I pour soapy water from the tub over me.
The last rinse.
It's Saturday night.
We're going to town.
I reach for the towel hanging on the nail.
I wrap it around me and dash upstairs to dress.
I'll get almost dry on the way.
Clean shirt.
Denim pants with only one patch.
Downstairs.
Supper is on the table.
Canned pork, fried potatoes, gravy, biscuits.
Everyone eats quickly.
It's almost seven.
The picture shows starts at seven-thirty.
We don't want to miss the comedy.
Or the serial before the main feature.
Perhaps a Tom Mix feature.
We won't know 'till it starts.
Mom says she'll do the dishes when we get home.

We pile into the car.
Arguing about who has to sit in the middle.
Dad drives slowly.
He has to compare all the cornfields with his.
I wish he would drive faster.
We park in front of Harry's Garage on Main Street.
Harry is Dad's brother who sells cars.
I have a dime for the show.
A nickel for popcorn.
So do the other kids.
Mom says to meet back at the car by ten.
The picture show starts in seven minutes.

We scatter.
I sit on the iron railing by the drug store.
Ronald comes along just in time.
We head for the show.
We decide to share one sack of popcorn.
That way we'll have a nickel for candy afterwards.
We sit behind some town girls by accident.
They pretend not to know we are there.
Anyway they have their own popcorn.
But it's just nice to be there.
The comedy is very funny and everyone laughs.
Mr. Barquist has to change reels before the feature.
He has only one projector.
So he has to change halfway through the feature too.
That gives us a chance to stretch.
We accidentally touch the girls in front of us.
They just giggle.
They probably think we did it on purpose.
The movie starts again.
Tom Mix does something I think I'll try sometime.
He swings down from his saddle
         and shoots from underneath his horse.
I forget now who he was shooting at.
But he hit whoever it was.

The show is over.
It's only nine-thirty.
Ronald and I sit on the railing again.
There is almost a full moon.
We talk.
We also wait to see if the girls will walk by.
They don't
so we decide to meet tomorrow and trap gophers.
I go back to the car.
Mom has bought groceries.
Dad is talking with Uncle Harry.
Pretty soon we drive home.
The car makes crunchy sounds on the gravel.
It's a wonderful feeling
         to go to town on Saturday night.

Duel in the Sun

Perhaps it was one day when we were bored.
Or maybe we'd been reading Robin Hood—
                    my friend and me.
I don't remember now.
Some reason anyway we settled on the crazy scheme
                    to have a duel.

We'd dress as knights of old
and see if one could knock the other off his horse.
Whoever won would get a prize—
some favorite thing the other owned
        like a slingshot or a rusty pocketknife.

We worked two weeks or more
            whenever we could find the time
to fashion costumes we would wear into the fray.

Each faceguard helmet was a work of art
                or so at least we thought.
We slit a length of stovepipe up the back
                    to form the base
and snipped four holes in front
                for eyes and nose and mouth.
We used two leather thongs to tie the gadget on.
Our chest protectors were much easier done.
We made two padded vests from straw-filled sacks
that tied behind our backs with binder twine.

We saved our legs from harm
by wearing rubber boots
and cut long strips of canvas cloth
            to wrap our arms.

A bamboo fishing pole cut six feet long
        became our warrior's lance.

At a glance you'd see our sturdy shields
were actually the same design and shape
as lids our mothers put on copper boilers
        for heating water on the stove
        each Monday when they washed the clothes.
We'd put them back in time for that.

We couldn't tell another soul
about the plans we'd made
to let the daring escapade unfold
            on Tuesday afternoon.
That seemed the wisest course somehow.
Mothers being who they are
would not allow such foolishness
                if they found out.

We had no doubt of that and yet
it seemed a shame a cheering crowd
would never stomp their feet and shout aloud
the name of one of us who would emerge
            the winner of our summer duel.
But then we also knew in truth
that each of us was just a little scared
                or worse than that
of what we planned to do so close to home.
Maybe it was just as well to stage the duel alone—
                at least the first time through.

When Tuesday came I hoped for rain
so I could then forget
                the whole darned thing.
Instead I'd make a giant circus swing
            up in the hayloft of the barn.
No harm could come of that I knew.

But Tuesday dawned all bright and clear.
No clouds appeared.
No voice suggested work to do.
No call from Ron to say he couldn't come.
I knew I had no choice.
I had to go ahead with plans so bravely made.

Ron showed up just shortly after one
and I could tell he wasn't feeling all that well.
Neither of us cared too much who won the duel
so long as we could save our pride
and keep from looking like a fool
                before the other one.

We talked about the rules we'd made.

Ron got the sorrel mare to ride
                    and I took Spot.
She had the easier stride
but he the faster of the two.
We'd ride bareback.
We knew the knights of old
            would never ride that way.
Still all in all
it was the safest thing to do.
That way
We'd fall straight off our charging steeds
and not get caught in saddle straps
or catch our feet in stirrup cups
                    and make a mess of things.

Once at the pasture site
we'd make some practice runs
to let the horses learn we said
just how to come full tilt one at the other.
And while we didn't say a thing
we knew a little practicing
might help us overcome the fright
                    we felt inside.

So it was that summer afternoon
                    when we were young—
two youthful knights bravely riding forth
                    to battle in the sun.
Stovepipe masks and padded suits.
Copper shields and bamboo spears.
Pounding hearts and sweaty hands.
Bravely riding forth with fear.
No turning back.
No saving face.
No place to hide.
No way with grace to stop the foolish game.
It must be played
            in order to survive with pride.

We meet mid-field
            the practice runs complete.
One last salute.

We turn and ride apart.
On count of ten we wheel again
        and close the gap at trotting speed.
Each lance makes contact with the other's shield
and brushes off—no damage done.
We both had won round one.

More bravely now
        we make a second run—a faster pace.
But just before we meet
        both horses shy away.
No contact made.
We've both survived to fight another day.

We rest our mounts
and take a firmer purchase on our shields.
The third and final moment has arrived.
This time we promise not to yield
                no matter what the price we pay.
We turn our gallant steeds once more
to make that final dash full speed.
We meet.
Our lances smash to smithereens
                against the copper shields
and each of us is shaken to the core.
With but a single thought
each drops his tools of war
and grabs ahold his horse's mane
to keep from falling off and forfeiting the game.

The duel is done.
We've kept the vows we've made.
We'll ride back to the house
        and see if Mom will make some lemonade.

Bike Rider

Perhaps Dad knew
      the way Dads know such things
that now and then we envied kids in town
because of shiny bikes they had to ride around.

It's true, of course,
the town kids envied us a lot
because of Spot that we could ride
      or in a pinch the sorrel mare.

In any case
Dad bought a bike in town one day
        and brought it home.
It was a beauty to behold.
No matter that the seat was gone
      one pedal broken off and lost
        both fenders bent
          the tires flat.

No harm in that we knew.
It was our bike—
the only bike we ever owned
and any farm kid worth his name
could fix it up as good as new.

The trouble was it didn't work that way.
Bob said it was too big for him.
Weldon always seemed to find
      a lot of other things to do.
Arline said that anyway
      it was a bike for boys.
So that left me in charge.

Oh, I took a stab at bike repair.
I found a board and carved a seat
almost as neat as what the real one
        might have been.
But then
there was no way to keep it fastened on.
The bolt I found to make a pedal from

had threads reversed in such a way
it took almost a day to figure out
                    it wouldn't work.
I patched the inner tubes
and pumped the tires with air
                until my face was blue.
Then in despair
I'd hear the air leak out again
        almost as fast as I had pumped it in.

Determined now to find a way
            to ride that cussed thing
I turned to far-out measures.
First off
I filled the tires with oats
and taped them to the rims real tight
                which seemed to work all right.
By pushing the contraption up a hill
            and standing on the pedal that remained
I found a way to lean way out
and coast it down again smart as you please.

Having mastered such a tricky ride
I was content to put the bike away
until the day when Dad had time to fix it right.
He never did.

Rainy Day

Early morning rain
      warm gentle soothing
whispering to me from outside the window—
secret messages
      pulling in opposite directions
      seductive and alluring.
"Close your eyes and sleep a little longer—
      it's too wet for work outside."
"Wake up and dress—
      the rain means freedom for the day."

I compromise.
I close my eyes and listen to the rain and plan.
I'll call Ron right after breakfast.
We'll ride the ponies
all the way to Squaw Creek and fish.

No.
Too far.
Besides Bob would want to tag along.

We'll hide in the feed house
      and smoke corn-silk cigarettes
      and tell naughty stories for an hour or so.

I know.
We'll catch the calves
      and have a Wild West rodeo.
Better yet.
We'll ask Dad if we can have those buggy wheels
      and make a two-wheeled cart for Spot to pull.

So many things to do
      so little time to choose.
This kind of summer rain could last 'till noon
              perhaps all day.
Long enough in any case to get away.

We could hunt rats beneath the crib
      or practice tightrope-walking in the barn
      or take the 22 and shoot at cans.

On the other hand
        we could spear frogs along the drainage ditch
        or make blowguns from hollow sticks
        or simply find a quiet place and talk.

Downstairs
I hear Dad shake the ashes from the stove.
He's up and knows it's raining too.
Any moment now I'll hear the call.
"Time to get up, boys.
It's raining out.
A perfect day for hoeing yellow burrs."

Monday Mornings

Each Monday morning was the same
unless the rain came pouring down
hard enough to drown a cat as Dad would say.
Otherwise
Mom set the day aside for washing clothes
and nothing in the whole wide world
could keep her from that weekly task.

We all pitched in to start the day.
Dad stoked the kitchen stove red hot
                and put the copper boiler on.
I'd fill the thing with pails of water
                taken from the cistern pump.
Like as not
I'd have to fill the washtubs too.

My brother didn't care for household chores
and there were always other things for him to do
                like cleaning out the barn manure.
While this was going on
the hired man made sure the Maytag's engine
was all oiled and filled with gas
so it would pop and start right off
                the minute Mom said go.

That done
we all cleared out 'till noon
and let Mom run her washday show
the way she wanted to.

She'd drop a load of dirty clothes
in water hot enough
to take the hide right off a hog.
Then quick as that
she'd start the agitator swishing
and dash inside the house
to finish up the breakfast dishes.

Back out in no time flat
she'd turn the wringer on

and use the washing stick to fish out clothes
                              too hot to touch by hand.
They'd squeeze between the wringer rolls
and splash into tub one to soak a bit
before Mom swung the wringer 'round
and sent them through again
                              to rinse in number two.
One more wringer turn from left to right
and then the rollers squeezed once more
            and dropped them in the basket on the floor.

On a run to save her time
she'd take the first batch out
and hang the clean damp clothes on wire lines
that stretched down through the yard—
            almost to the road in fact.

Then back again
to start the process with the second load
followed by loads three and four
as though someone
had put a curse on dirty clothes—or worse.

By going flat out as she did
she'd finish up by half past ten
and then she'd use her extra time
to scrub the wash-house floor
the porch
and then the sidewalk going from the door.
I guess she hated dirt and grime
about as much as anyone you'd find
                              when we were growing up.

She'd work like that all morning long
and yet when we came in to eat at noon
she'd have the kitchen table set
            and dinner ready on the stove.
Then like as not
            as we were bolting down our food
she'd tell some funny joke to make us laugh.

Once she'd shooed us from the house
            and got the dishes done and put away

she'd take the first clothes off the line
and start in ironing to finish up her day.

She'd put two flatirons on the stove
                    to heat just right
and set the ironing board in such a way
that she'd have light
and still could catch what little breeze
                    came through the house.
There she'd be 'till four o'clock at least.
She'd fit one iron hot enough to burn
into a handle gadget that she had
and use it for a spell until it cooled
and then return it to the spot atop the stove
                    and take another one in turn.

When evening came
she never talked about the work she'd done
or how hard life could be for one
                    who had to be a farmer's wife.
More likely she'd be laughing gay
and talking of the dance
            coming up on Saturday.

Vaccinating Pigs

One night at supper time
we'd get the word from Dad.
"Doc Wilder's coming by tomorrow," he'd say.
"Doc said he'd be here anyway by ten
                    to vaccinate the pigs.
We'll have to get them penned by nine
in case he's runnin' way ahead of time."

We knew right then
tomorrow would be hot as all get out.
It always was when Doc came by to do the pigs.

Next day we'd have the morning chores all done
by half past six or so
and then we'd set about to ready everything
for Doc's performance in the ring.

Each of us would pick a favorite stick
to drive two hundred adolescent pigs
                    all roaming free
into the hog-house lot.

Once there
we'd run about a fourth the herd
                    some fifty head
into the holding pens inside the house
and wait for Doc to come.

I never thought I'd like to be a vet
and yet I always thought Doc Wilder
            was a special sort of man.
He wore a perky mustache on his lip
                    I thought was keen
and had a twinkle in his eye most of the time.
I never saw him mean or out of sorts
no matter how much cause there might have been.
He never had boys of his own.

I always felt real good
when Doc came driving through the gate
                    most likely half an hour late

113

but then we never thought he'd be on time.
He never was.
It never made a speck of difference in my mind.
Being late in no way changed important things
            like how he smelled of iodine and liniment
            and all the other kinds of medicines he used.
He'd pull on rubber boots and gab awhile
                    about how hot the day.
That done
he'd hand his dusty doctor's bag to me
            and grab a box of serum bottles
            from the back seat of his Chevrolet.
Dad would take a second box or two
and lead the way out through the gate
to where the day's routine would start.

Doc picked a corner of the teeming pen
                    to set up shop.
He had a corner shelf to hold supplies—
            a dauber for his iodine
            bottles filled with serum
            and two mean-looking hypodermic things
            that squirted vaccine underneath the skin.
A V-shaped wooden trough
            fastened to the top board of the pen
would hold a squirming pig face up
when his turn came to feel the needle going in.

When Doc was ready for the show to start
he'd plant his feet real firm and say
"Boys, bring me a pig. Let's go."
I'd grab a pig hind leg or fore
                    no matter which
and lift him from the floor into the trough
and trap his snout beneath a leather thong
            before he knew just what was going on.
Doc smeared a dab of iodine
            and jammed the needle in to give the shot.
Weldon would be right behind
            holding tight the pig he'd caught
then Dad

114

then me again
until we'd finished with all fifty in the lot
and only had a hundred fifty more to go.

With luck we'd finish up by noon
                or shortly after that.
Good thing we did.
It got so hot and dusty in the place
                you couldn't breathe.
And once you let your arms hang down
you couldn't hardly lift them up again
                and that's a fact.

When we came to the house to eat
Mom had a tub of water warming in the sun
and basins on the bench outside for us to use.
We'd strip down to our waists
and scrub our hides until they hurt
        to wash away the hog-house dirt.

In actual fact it didn't do much good.
The stench remained
        when we marched in the house
        to eat the spareribs Mom had fixed.
She'd sniff the air and then proclaim
"You men smell just like a bunch of pigs."
I guess we did
but we would put the blame on Doc.
He'd only laugh and claim he didn't smell a thing
except he'd like another slab of spareribs please.

We loved ol' Doc for that.

Manure Haulers

How should one describe a chore
that took the time of all of us
before late summer turned to fall?
That was the time of year
      three weeks at least or more
when we cleaned barns and feedlots of manure.

Take a hundred head of steers
      plus twice as many pigs
and put them in a feeding lot that's not too big.
Fill five long bunks two times a day
      with silage first and then ear corn.
Then jam four wooden racks with clover hay.
Two times a week at least
spread straw twelve inches deep
      all through the pole-type barn
so they can get their beauty sleep.

Do all that for seven months
      while steers get fat and pigs mature
and you've got several hundred tons
of plain old animal manure to haul away.

We took a certain family pride
in cleaning barns and feeding lots
of refuse from the year now gone
to make them ready for the year to come.
All five of us were needed for the job—
the five consisting of my Dad
      three sons and Lawrence the hired man.

We'd spend day one just making sure
those three old spreaders were in tune.
We'd check the chains and power gears
and replace all the broken platform slats.
The platform moved on rollers
shoving back the load from front to rear
where next a whirling beater sort of thing
would catch it up and fling it back
        to scatter on the field.

116

Here's how the work would go
with three boys driving chariots of gold
                    and two men helping load.

We'd all pitch in to fill rig one
and send it down the road
to where the field a half a mile away
          was waiting for this offering.
When it was on its way
rig two would get its fill and rumble forth
to meet rig one now heading home
                    and empty of its load.
Rig three would start to make its run
the minute number one came through the gate.

That's mainly how it was
                as I remember now
and yet somehow
I've failed to capture the allure
when one of summer's last demands
involved our hauling out manure.

Working as a team was part of it.
But there was more.
The lazy rides
          out to the fields and back again
gave freedom to the mind to dream
about those things boys dream about.
The horses knew the route without command.
I'd settle back
                reins loosely held in hand
and dream about the wondrous things I'd do
                    when I became a man.
I'd find a secret way to fly—
          better than that hawk up there.
I'd join the F.B.I.
I'd build the fastest car of any of its day
          and race it sixty miles an hour anyway.
I'd be a movie star and play Tarzan.
I'd be the fastest man who ever ran a mile.
I'd fly around the world alone and win acclaim
          the way that Lindy did when he came home.

117

I'd take a whirl at climbing mountains in Tibet.
And you can bet
        I'd have the prettiest girl in town.

We're at the field.
The horses stop and look around.
It's time to be a boy again
           and turn the spreader on.

Cowboy Suit

He smiled out from the page
      this handsome lad of eight or ten
around my size and age at any rate
and dressed in just the finest cowboy suit
            Sears Roebuck ever made.

A cotton shirt of khaki tan
      with white-stitched seams.
An imitation leather vest
      a darker shade.
Khaki pants to match the shirt
      complete with oilcloth chaps.
A wide-brimmed cowboy hat.
A woven belt—
      the buckle looked like brass.
Two holsters and a pair of guns—
      Colt .45's at least.
And then to top the outfit off
      a pair of shiny cowboy spurs
      for breaking broncs and riding fast.

Sears sent out the catalog in spring.
I'd turned that page a thousand times
      and led another kind of life in fantasy.
I'd pull my hat low down
      and walk like movie cowboys do.
I'd draw my guns and fire quick
      to get some hombre on the loose.
I'd rope a wild horse in the hills
      and break him in so he'd be mine.
If I just had that suit,
      I'd be the finest cowboy of all time.

Each day I coaxed and promised Mom
if she'd just send that order off to Sears
      somehow I'd earn the money that it cost.
I'd weed the garden good and gather eggs.
I'd churn the butter every week
      and help her beat the rugs.

I'd fill the water pail each day
        and carry in the coal and cobs.
In fact, I'd do most anything she asked.

It's true that in the lower corner of the page
Sears did display an Indian suit at cheaper price.
I'd have no part of that.
I did agree it was the sort of thing
my brother Bob would like—
        he being just a kid.

As things turned out
Mom sent the order off for both.
She never made it clear
        the kind of work that Bob would do.

Right after that
        no later than a day or two
I started in to wait.
Bob also played the waiting game.
We'd find a vantage point down by the gate
pretending we had other things to do
        until the mailman came along.
We'd whittle sticks or throw stones at a post.
We'd look real hard for four-leaf clovers
                in the yard.
We'd do most anything until we heard
the mailman's car come chugging down the road.
Each time we'd just about explode with hope
that this would be the day he'd stop and grin
and call us to the car
        to get the package he had brought.
But every day he'd only pause
and put the daily papers in the box
and drive on down the road
                without a backward glance.
If he'd looked back
he would have seen a would-be cowboy
                and an Indian scout
trudging head down toward the house.

For weeks that same charade took place
with only minor variations in the theme.

And then the magic moment came—
      the day we knew our world
      would never be the same old world again.
Playing casual as before
we heard the mailman stop outside the gate.
From a corner of my eye
I saw him put the papers in the box.
But then the sequence changed.
The car stayed where it was and didn't drive away.
Instead we heard the mailman toot his horn
      and when we turned
      he called and said real serious like
"You boys expecting anything from Sears?"
We tried to act surprised
but we were through that gate in nothing flat.
He handed us a big brown package tied with string
and said he sort of thought it might contain
            a thing or two for us.
Then he laughed and said good luck
      or something nice like that
and we said thanks and tore back to the house.

Mom opened up that package pretty fast
but not as fast as Bob and me
had stripped down to our B.V.D.'s.
Bob got dressed up first
      he being youngest of the pair
and I could see right off
that plain old Indian suit fit him real good.
He looked just like an Indian chief
except he had blue eyes
      and long blond curly hair.

There were some minor problems I'll admit
when my turn came to get into my cowboy suit.
First off
the khaki shirt with white-stitched seams
         fit just a bit too soon.
No matter how I scrunched inside
my gangling arms were longer than the sleeves
leaving naked wrists I couldn't hide.

121

The matching pants with oilcloth chaps
fit fine around the waist
but stopped a good four inches short
        from where a cowboy's cuffs should be
and left my bony ankles in plain view
                    for all the world to see.

The holsters and the guns were there
but even they seemed smaller than the ones
on page four ninety-three of Sears.

Mom tried to take the blame.
She said she guessed I'd grown
                    more than she realized.
She thought we'd better send it back
                    and get a larger size.
I maintained it fit just fine
and maybe it would stretch a bit with time.
In any case
I wore that suit for three straight weeks
                playing make-believe it fit.
Then one day came and I faced up to truth.
The suit no matter what was just too small.
I took it off and donned my overalls again
and after that
I passed the word around
that I was just too darned grown up
                to play such silly cowboy games.

Fall

It is like this in fall it seems to me.
Reminders to us all of how life is
                and how life has to be.
Burning moments of delight.
Other moments of despair.
Happiness the background hue.
But always too
        those polka dots of yearning.

A Special Time

Fall is such a special time
        when one is growing up a boy.
I don't know all the reasons why
        nor am I able to explain it all.
A special time
        for all the reasons writers write about.
The autumn rains.
The golden leaves that blaze so beautifully
                before they gently fall.
The distant haze.
The way the birds behave
        before they say good-by and leave.
The dusty goldenrod.
The way the ripened milkweed pods
        send fleecy clouds into the wind.
The morning light.
The lazy final flight of bumblebees
                so faintly heard.
The start of school.
The cool of early morning
        when we're doing chores.

But more than anything it seems to me
it is the way a field of ripened corn
        conveys the meaning of it all.
Standing stately tall in ordered rows
each stalk expresses in its way
how life begins
        and how it must be lived
                and how it now can end
                        with pride and dignity.
Once given birth so early in the spring
        it takes its nourishment from earth
                and sips the rain.
It greets each new day's rising sun
        until in early summer it becomes
                an adolescent of the world.
Growing tall and rangy strong
its leafy arms embrace the warmth

until it can become a young adult
to foster new life of its own.
Now in fall
it greets the twilight of its years
unbowed unscorned
and offers to the world its gift of life—
a golden yellow ear of corn
so others next year may be born.

It is like this in fall it seems to me.
Reminders to us all of how life is
and how life has to be.
The warmth of summer's sun.
The chill of winter winds to come.
The beauty of the trees with golden hair.
Their drabness when once shorn of leaves
and bare.
Burning moments of delight.
Other moments of despair.
Happiness the background hue.
But always too
those polka dots of yearning.

Fall is such a special time
when one is growing up a boy.

Garden Center School

It's gone now.
Knocked down at auction I suppose
     the highest bidder paying half its worth.
Moved away from where it stood.
Converted to a bin or crib perhaps
        or torn apart for scrap.
The coal house thrown in to sweeten up the deal.

Gone now anyway.
Outdated.
No longer needed once the school consolidated
          sometime after World War II.
There being so few kids in any case.
The land sold too I would assume
       an acre more or less
making room to grow more corn and soybeans.

A stranger whizzing by would never know.
He'd never have a clue
that Garden Center School was gone.
Its land producing now
     an extra load of corn or two.
And anyway
that stranger wouldn't likely care
that Garden Center School was where all kids
who lived around a two-mile square
learned how to read and write and spell
       and more than that.
They learned the capitals of states
all flowing rivers of the land
all major history dates
     and how fine glass is made of sand.
They learned about the stars
and how the Pilgrims came
and how Abe Lincoln freed the slaves.
They learned the way the West was won
     and just how Custer met his fate.
Kids learned an awful lot of things
in grades from one through eight
       at Garden Center School.

You can't expect a fancy plaque
            where two roads intersect
that tells you where the school house stood.
Right over there it was—
just north of where the drainage ditch
cuts south and slices through Cliff Taylor's land.

You'll never see a monument of stone
            in tribute to the weeping willow tree.
It was the only play equipment
            the school board ever owned.
There is no sign
            with letters etched in gold
that tells the basic facts about the place.
A saving grace, perhaps.
What could it say?
Who would have read it anyway
            if these had been the words:

Garden Center School once claimed
                this corner of the world.
A one-room frame design
            with entrance hall
where all along one wall you'd find
an eight-inch shelf for dinner pails
                and underneath
two rows of nails for hanging coats and
            caps and extra overalls.
There too
a wooden stand to hold the water can
            one dipper used by all
and a basin where you washed your hands
            when coming in from playing ball.
One corner set aside for gopher traps
and homemade kites and braided leather straps
as well as other precious things like that
                kids seem to have.

Inside the scene shaped up like this:
The row of windows on the south
let in the natural light—

the only kind of light there was in fact
        and not too much of that on rainy days.
Us kids of course all faced the other way
            occupying as we did
six rows of well-carved wooden desks
            five desks per row.
There was a stage—six inches raised—
where teacher sat behind her desk
and up in front of that the recitation bench
            where all the classes met.
The monstrous coal-fired heating stove
        squatted in one corner of the room.
Cold and sullen when it had no role to play
        but a warm and friendly giant
        when filled with burning coal.

Each day the school bell rang at ten 'till nine.
That way
you had ten minutes' time to get inside
and hang your jacket on a hook
before the teacher took the roll.
You'd better answer "here" real clear
when teacher called your name
or else you'd have to pay a heavy price
            for being late.
You'd get a black mark on your chart
and have to stay inside when recess came.
Too many marks meant staying in at noon as well
and doing chores like wiping clean the slate
        or getting coal or sweeping floors
        or doing other silly things like that.

Once all of us had answered "here"
we'd stand and pledge allegiance to the flag
and sing "America the Beautiful" so loud
            it hurt your ears.

That done
we'd hope the best was yet to come
when teacher might decide to read
        another chapter in the book.

It might be *Huckleberry Finn* this time
　　　　or *Robin Hood* or even *Moby-Dick*
that keeps us spellbound in our seats
　　　　'till half past nine
and teaches us our love for books.

The book is closed and put away.
There is a murmur of regret
but other learning must begin.
The teacher calls each class in turn.
"Fourth grade arithmetic,
　　　　turn, stand, and pass."
"Sixth grade geography,
　　　　turn, stand, and pass."
"First grade reading,
　　　　turn, stand, and pass."
With such commands in quiet tones
　　　　at twenty-minute intervals
all Garden Center scholars of a given grade
　　　　in gingham frocks or overalls
parade up to the recitation bench
　　　　and empty out their minds.
What is the capital of Vermont?
How much is six times nine?
What is the longest river in the world?
Who settled Jamestown—when and where?
Recite your favorite nursery rhyme.
What did Hiawatha do?
How many feet make up a mile?
What makes a fire burn?
See if you can count to ten.

While other grades held center stage
you listened with one ear
to things you'd learned the year before
　　　　or things you'd have to know next year.

Now looking back
I wonder if we were so smart
to heap such ridicule on how kids learned
　　　　attending one-room country schools.

Silage Makers

Only a whispered sound at first.
A plaintive murmur
        drifting through the open door.
Lonesome and sad.

I couldn't be sure.
Sitting there daydreaming.
In the eighth grade row of Garden Center School
        pretending to read my history book
        on a Friday afternoon.

Dad said they wouldn't start today.
Not 'till Saturday morning anyway.

More alert now.
I listen for the sound to come again.
A low and mournful wail
        faintly from a distance.
Like the wind
        testing a window partly open.
But different.
Unlike any other sound in the world.
Louder for a moment
        a higher pitch—then low again
like gentle waves of anguish
        turning defiant
                then fading to a softer plea.

No doubting now.
The men have come to fill the silo by the barn.
I'm a quarter-mile away in school.
I should be home.

I should be home to stand up close
and listen to the throaty moan
the silage cutter makes
as it takes stalks of corn
        and chops them fine.
Then like a cyclone on the loose
it blows the silage through a pipe

up to the silo top
and lets it fall inside
gentle as a summer rain.

I should be home
and if the hired man had other things to do
I'd get to run the dangerous machine
for just a little while at least
        if Mom were not around to see.

I should be home to work out in the field
helping men take bundles tied with twine
and toss them on those flatbed racks
        for transport to the ravenous machine.

I should be home
inside the silo with my Dad
making sure the silage as it falls
gets tramped real hard to pack it down
so it won't mold
before we feed it to the steers
        all winter long.

I should be home
to keep the tractor filled with gas
and oil the cutter's gears
and play the role of power engineer.

I should be home.
A man of twelve and growing strong
has no real business here in school
when silo-filling's going on.

The moaning wail now fades and dies.
A buzzing fly the only sound.
Perhaps they've finished for the day.
A practice run
to make sure things are working well.
Tomorrow is the day we'll truly start
                just like Dad said.

Tomorrow is a Saturday
        and I'll be home.

Chicken Catchers

One morning sure as anything
        right after we'd had frost
Mom would put her coffee down
        and say to Dad—
"Now, Ben, tonight you men have got
to help me put the chickens in.
They're going to freeze out there
        roosting in the trees."

Chickens were Mom's sole responsibility.
They didn't rate too high with Dad
        compared to raising hogs each year
        and feeding white-faced Hereford steers.

Once those chicks had feathered out
        as adolescent birds
Mom turned them loose
and let them forage for themselves.

During summer
she would catch a rooster once a week
for frying as a Sunday dinner treat.
Otherwise
the whole flock roamed scot-free by day
and stayed out of harm's way at night
by roosting in the trees.
They didn't grow too fast that way
but on the other hand
Mom didn't pay out cash for chicken feed.
Anyway that's how it was
when Mom put out her call for help
one morning early in the fall.

We knew of course
there were a lot of other things to do
before the crew fanned out at night
to gather in the whole darned flock
        and separate the pullets from the cocks.
First thing
someone had to go to town for coops

so we could clear the laying house
        of last year's laying hens.
Once penned
we'd take them back to town for sale
to end up I would guess
        in cans of Campbell's chicken soup.
That done
we'd have to clean the house
and soak most everything with creosote
        to kill the lice and mites.

Right after supper
        as soon as it was dark outside
we'd organize in two-man teams
to start the chicken-catching enterprise.
One team would take the grove out east
        and sweep it clean of birds.
Another pair would search the barn
        and all the other buildings on the farm.
Team number three pursued the strays
        when they escaped the other two.
Mom supervised.
She sorted all the birds when they arrived.
She'd put the pullets in the laying house
to earn their winter's keep by laying eggs.
The cockerels spent the night in coops
                until tomorrow's sale.

Catching chickens after dark
is something of a work of art
no matter what some people say.
Here's what you do.
Shine a flashlight in the tree
until you spot a roosting bird asleep.
Then like a stealthy thief
sneak underneath its perch
and gently lift it down before it squawks
and scares the other birds.
Then quickly put it in a gunny sack
                your partner holds.
Without a word

135

move on to still another sleeping bird
and do the same until the sack is full.

Birds on branches lowest down
are fairly easy to retrieve.
But some will always choose
choice perches higher in the trees
                 to test your catching skill.
For these
you take a length of heavy wire
                 number nine will work
and bend one end into a curving hook.
With this device in hand
climb the tree part way
and stand where you can snare one leg
and swing the bird head down into the sack.

Once Mom was sure we'd caught the lot
she'd hurry to the house at ten
                 or later still
to light the lamps
and make hot cocoa on the stove
to take the chill away when we came in.

I hope I haven't dwelt too long
on such an ordinary task
as helping Mom catch chickens when she asked.
It isn't much to write about
                 not grand at all
and yet it was a special thing
                 we did each fall.

Corn Harvest

I am awake.
Night's dark and cold await the sun.
I lie there in the warm
               knowing that it's Saturday.
Knowing that today we'll start to harvest corn.

My brothers sleep.
Outside
a sliver of a moon keeps company with stars.
There in the dark
               I wait for day to come.

A flicker of first light
          sifting through the chimney grate
casts ghostly shadows on the ceiling of my room.
A single lamp's been lighted
in the living room below.
Dad lights the stove
and soon a glowing fire
sends welcome messages to me.
In darkness still
          a morning has arrived.
It's harvest time.
It's good to be alive on such a day.

I leave my bed and dress
to hurry down
and go outside to test the cold
and check the eastern sky
               for any trace of dawn.
Glad now there's only dark
where morning light will come.

Our lanterns show the way
and cast long striding shadows out
           keeping pace
as men and boys walk toward the barn
to do the morning chores.

Hanging now from pegs inside the barn
the lanterns softly light another world—

the magic world of animals who wait
for men to come to share the muted sounds
                    the special warmth
the subtle fragrance I cannot describe.

In quietness the chores are done.
Cows are fed their hay and milked.
Horses given oats and corn and curried clean
        before they don their leather garb
                    to start the day.

Reluctantly
we leave the gentle comfort of this place
and step into the chill outside
to feel the subtle changes being made
as morning gives the blackness of the night
                    a faintly lighter shade.
The windmill stands in silent silhouette
            against the sky
serving as a reference point perhaps
for flocks of wild geese flying south again
                from where they've been.
There by the crib four wagons wait.
All now adorned in awkward grace
with layered wooden shields
against which men will fling
the golden ears of corn
            soon taken from the fields.

We hurry then.
A lighted kitchen window
shows the way along the path
that leads us through the gate and to the house
where Mom awaits five hungry men.
She has the table loaded down—
            fried eggs
            big cuts of ham
            a pan of baking-powder biscuits
            pork gravy
            crisp pancakes smeared with jam
            and coffee boiling hot
            served from a gallon coffee pot.

138

We feast
and then as morning light appears
we grab our husking gear and hurry to the barn
to hitch our teams and move out down the road.
There a field of corn awaits our harvest race
            against the coming winter storms.

Our uniforms are suited for the chore.
The layered look
            before it made the fashion books.
Two pairs of overalls to start
            one coming off as soon as we get hot.
A cotton shirt with extra sleeves pinned on
                        to save on wear.
A denim jacket flannel lined.
Two pairs of socks inside thick heavy shoes.
One pair of two-thumbed cotton gloves
            sized right for either boy or man.
A vicious looking husking hook
            with leather straps to tie around my hand.

It's almost light when we arrive.
The night clouds now a pinkish white.
The grey-brown stalks stand tall
            in long straight rows
heads bowed but proud
            as though each knows the time has come
            to make its final offering
                        to justify its time on earth.
Their gifts hang down from slender stems.
Bright yellow ears of corn
that Nature wrapped in layered sheaths
                        first young and green
but now an aging greyish brown
                        with wrinkled skin.

I turn my team astride a barren row.
Dad picked it early in the week
            to open up the field and check the yield.
The second row he picked is next
            and I will husk the two rows after that.
Weldon follows me and takes two more.

140

His team astride a standing row I've picked.
Then Dad and then the hired man.
The caravan of four
      moves slowly through the standing field.

It takes a little time
before the rhythm of the task returns.
Once it does
my mind is free to roam at will.
My arms and hands work automatically
to fill the wagon box with corn.

I stoop and let my left hand grasp a covered ear
                down by the tip
and with my right-hand husking hook
I rip the covering bare along one side
and hold the partly naked ear
until my left hand strips away the rest.
My right hand goes to work again.
It breaks the stem that holds the ear
              now bare
and flings the gift of gleaming gold
against the wagon's bangboard shield
from where it falls to join the hoard
              already there.
A turn to left head down.
Another stalk to glean.
A step ahead between two more.
First right then left.
The same routine.
Pull back the husks then break then fling.
Pull back the husks then break then fling.
On command the horses move ahead
              four steps or five
              then stop.
I don't look up.
Pull back the husks then break then fling.
My spirits sing.
It's great to be alive
and working like a man at harvest time.

141

I set a goal.
I'll have a forty-bushel load husked clean
            before the sun announces noon.
Each bushel claims a hundred ears or more.
This means that in my role as man
I must repeat four thousand times
the sequence of my husking act.
Pull back the husks then break then fling.
Four seconds have elapsed.
Pull back the husks then break then fling.
Four seconds more.

And then it's noon.
All wagons pull out from their rows
                and head for home.
Up ahead I hear Lawrence sing
                "The Wabash Cannonball."
The sun is warm.
I'm feeling good.
I have a forty-bushel load
to represent the work I've done.

Now one by one we wait our turn
to unload all our hard-earned loot.
The elevator carries it aloft
and drops it through the chute
into the storage vault we call the crib.

Corn harvest has begun.

The Plowman

A thousand years it seemed
I'd waited for this moment to arrive.
The day in fall
when Dad would think me old enough
to drive the tractor all alone
and take my turn at helping plow.

Right now I don't recall just when it was
that Dad decided to relent
and let a tractor replace horses on the plow.
I'd guess
he bought the tractor at some auction sale
                        well used and second hand
but worth the modest price he paid at that.

Three seasons of the year
it sulked in brooding grease-stained solitude
there in the grove of trees
ignoring winter's snow and spring's fresh rain
                        and summer's breeze.

Sulking there alone.
Ignored by everyone.
Waiting for the days of fall to come
        when it would be the pampered one.

Right after harvesting was done
we'd change its oil and feed it fuel
        and grease all moving parts
before we spun the starting crank
to coax it back to life.
It could be stubborn as a mule at times.
It'd stand there on its spindly iron wheels
        lug toes buried in the sod
and never budge or say a word.
We'd check the spark
        and fiddle with the carburetor valves.
We'd make appeals in barnyard terms
        and crank some more.
Then we'd hear a snort or two

143

that finally settled in a throaty roar.
The good old Avery was a friend again.

I worked a year or two I guess
as chief assistant to the hired man.
That way I learned to drive the clumsy thing
                    and hone my plowing skills
while serving under his command.
After school
I'd scoot out to the field and hitch a ride.
I'd watch the way he used one hand to steer
and note just how he turned around
to make adjustments on the plow.
He took great pride in making sure
each plowshare claimed its proper slice
before it lifted up the rich black earth
and curled it back upon itself.

My time arrived one day when I was twelve.
Dad allowed that I was strong enough
            to drive the rig alone.

I acted calm all during morning chores
so everyone would understand
            that plowing all alone
            was something of a bore.

After breakfast—eggs and ham—
I put my denim jacket on
and donned a pair of leather gloves
                    to look the part.

Outside
I filled the tractor tank with gas
                    and checked the oil
and prayed the stubborn thing would start
when I first turned the crank.
It did.
I climbed astride the iron seat and shifted gears.
Without a backward glance
I headed out the driveway gate and down the road.

Once in the field
I had the world all to myself

shared only with the wind and sun
and flights of blackbirds seeking worms.

With courage now
I turned my powerful machine upfield
and reached behind to trip the plow.
It sliced into the land
that had so recently in summer been
a golden field of grain.
Two shining moldboard shields
formed overlapping waves of rich black loam
curling up and cresting
and falling back again in long continuous rows
like worried frowns upon the face of earth.

The sun was warm across my back.
I felt the breeze
and watched the earth turn black.
I sang and shouted out.
I was the captain of the ship.
I was the master of my fate.
I was a king upon a throne.
But more than anything
I was a plowman all alone.

Thanksgiving

Thanksgiving anymore
just doesn't seem the same.
But then so few things are.
It doesn't seem to me we get the thrill
we used to get at our Thanksgiving time.

Here's how it was.

Some Sunday after church
        before November got too far along
we'd all pile in the Model-T
and head out to the turkey farm.
Once there
we'd buy a fancy-strutting bird
and tie his feet and put him in a gunny sack.
We'd cart him home
        and place him in a special pen we'd built.

All through the month
we'd fatten him on oats and corn and sour milk.
In return
he'd strut and fluff his feathers out
and lecture everyone around in turkey talk.
The only trouble was
he got to be a special friend.

Thanksgiving week Mom cleaned the house
        and opened up those parlor doors
                to honor Uncle Vern.
He would arrive by train at night
                along with wife Lorraine
from way out west somewhere
and everything in sight got cleaned before they came.

Wednesday was a mixed-up day for me
                sitting there in school.
A day of wild anticipation
        but with a touch of sadness too.
I knew when I got home at four
there'd be only silence
        coming from the turkey pen.

146

I never asked what happened to my friend.
It had to be that way.
Tomorrow was Thanksgiving Day.
Anyway it's just as well to learn
                    when one is young
that pleasure seldom can be earned
without a little sadness thrown in.

I'd find my spirits soaring high again
the moment I walked in the kitchen door
and let my senses be aware of what was going on.
If I'd been blind
I swear I would have known
                    it was Thanksgiving time.
So many rich aromas hit my head from everywhere.
From over there
the yeasty smell of baking bread.
A quarter turn
and even though my eyes were closed
my nose could lead me to the pumpkin pies
          taken from the still-hot stove.
Another turn
and from some far-off land
the magic scent of spices rare
that turned Mom's turkey dressing
                    into such fancy fare.

I always woke up feeling good Thanksgiving Day.
From down below
I'd hear warm friendly sounds.
Mom singing low some lilting song
as she prepared to put the turkey on
but stopping now and then to talk with Dad.
I couldn't always tell just what they said.
Dad's fire burning in the stove
warning in advance about the call for chores.
I'd lie there warm
and let my mind anticipate
                    the moments of the day.

147

I'd give each cow an extra ear of corn
        and maybe just a little extra hay.
After all this was their day as well.
I'd feed the cats whole milk instead of skim.
I'd turn the separator crank full speed
        to turn out thick rich cream we'd need.
I'd show my Uncle Vern the two new calves
and then I'd let him take my .22
        to try his hand at shooting cans.
I'd listen to my Aunt Lorraine
tell Mom about the fun they had
        riding on the train.
I'd watch Mom work and then conclude
        we couldn't even sample all that food.
Roast turkey as the featured course
                along with turkey dressing
potatoes—mashed and creamy white
                topped off with rich milk gravy
applesauce and acorn squash
scalloped corn and green string-beans
candied yams and red cranberries
homemade bread and twisted rolls
pumpkin pie—whipped cream on top.

I'd hear Dad call
"Come on you boys. It's time to go.
Thanksgiving's here."

As if we didn't know.

Chicken Thieves

Talk in town on Saturday night.
Rumors mostly.
Heard in Wing's Barber Shop.
Hard not to believe.
Near Stratford.
Chicken thieves had hit four farmers.
Took every bird around.
No one heard a sound.
That's how smart they were.
Like as not a thieving ring from out of state.
And yet
they seemed to know the territory pretty well.
No way to tell for sure.

Every fall around this time
the talk would be the same.
We'd wait excitedly for news to get around
about the only real good rural crime
there was to talk about.

This year we talked at supper time.
We made elaborate plans.
We'd catch the culprits in the act
if they should come around our place
                to steal our laying hens.

First thing
we burglar-proofed the chicken house
by putting on a brand-new lock
                that fastened with a key.
And then we did a second thing.
Each night we stretched a length of twine
across the path most likely used
                by anyone with thievery in mind.
One end fastened to a bucket filled with cans
                designed to fall and make an awful din
                if any would-be chicken thief walked in.
We figured once he heard the crash
he'd take off like the wind
and we'd come storming after him.

We stayed alert each night for any sight
                    or any sound
that didn't seem just right.
The moment we thought anything amiss
we turned out all the lamps
                    as though we'd gone to bed
and sat beside the windows looking out.
We listened for the slightest sound
and strained our eyes to see beyond the dark.
We whispered back and forth across the room
checking out all clues we thought we saw
                    even though
imagination has a way of playing funny tricks.
Did the shadow of that tree
conceal a crouching man?
I saw him move—I'm sure I did.
Or was it just the branches moving in the wind?

A car drives slowly by and stops
                    out there beyond the grove of trees.
Its lights go off.
That could be what we're waiting for.
It's hard to see.
Our hearts begin to pick up speed.
Five minutes pass—then ten.
There is no sound.
And then the car starts up.
The lights go on.
It moves on down the road again.
We laugh and make a guess.
What couple driving out from town
had stopped to pet a bit
not knowing they were seen
                    as likely chicken thieves?
Each year night after night
we played the waiting game a week or two.
But no thieves ever came.

I wonder what we might have done
                    if they had come.

Road Builders

His name was Mark.
A boy about my age but smaller built.
The only boy who for a time
I thought I'd like to be
          because of how his family lived.

His father made a living building roads.
A giant of a man.
Tall.
Black beard and heavy arms
               with eyes as dark as prunes.
He had a way with mules and for his work
he must have had a string of twenty anyway.

Mark's mother—small but whispery strong.
The quiet type.
Not a bit like Mom who liked to talk a lot.
Not like that at all but nice in any case.

Word came in the spring.
The old dirt road that passed our place
would soon be just a memory.
And just as well.
A narrow, dust-choked thoroughfare at times
                         until it rained.
Then it soon became
an oozing muddy lane one couldn't drive
          even with the best of tire chains.

A different kind of road would take its place.
A fancy high-grade job
well drained with deep-cut ditches on each side
          and tons of coarse road gravel on the top.
It would be the kind of farm-to-market road
the politicians talked about before election time.

We'd heard the talk
but never thought they had our road in mind.

Mark's Dad was hired on to build the road
                    some eight miles long

152

and everybody said he'd do it right—
                    the way it should be done.

That's how it was
            as summer turned to fall
that I met Mark
and why it was that we were friends.
By then the building crew was near at hand.
They'd started out at Jewell that spring
                    some five miles east
                            and headed west.
They had three miles to go to finish up
before an early winter snow would call a halt.

A corner of our pasture land
became base camp for mules and men
                    working on the road
and there I was to see
the first real mobile home I'd ever seen.
A giant box on iron wheels
it moved most anywhere behind a team of mules.
Inside there was a single coal-fired stove
            for cooking and for keeping warm
a bed
            a cot for Mark
                    one table and four chairs.
There was a row of nails along one wall
                    for hanging clothes.
Another row across the room
                    for hanging pots and pans.
A narrow wooden bench along the end
held basins and a tub for washing up.
It wasn't much to see.
But it could move from place to place.
That was enough for me.

Mark's folks stopped by soon after they arrived
to buy some milk and eggs and other things.
Mom said I should be Mark's friend.
I said I'd try.
I'd never had a stranger as a friend before.

At first we sort of looked up at the sky
and kicked the dirt and threw round stones at cans
        trying not to look each other in the eye.
And then Mark said he had a pony of his own.
I had Spot to ride.
So we agreed to meet next day
                right after I got out of school
and ride to where Mark's Dad
was working on the road.

Being on the move so much
Mark didn't have to be in school.
His mother gave him all the learning that he got.
I thought that was just about
the best thing in the world.
The closer we became as friends
the more it seemed to me
that living in a house on wheels
                and being taught at home
surely was the grandest way to live—
                the ultimate in being free.

I thought that way for sure
until they finished up the road
        much later in the fall.

That day they closed up camp
and packed their things
and moved the house away to some new place.
I knew that Mark and I might never meet again.
We never did.

Friendships ought to last more days than that.

Potato Diggers

Some probably believe
that I perceived all things as fun
when I was young and growing up
        a farm boy in the olden days
as my kids used to say in jest
when they themselves were young.

That's not exactly how it was.
But when you reach September of your years
you have the right to choose
        those best times to remember.
That's what I've done.
But if I try I can recall some jobs of fall
that didn't seem much fun at all
        coming as they did on Saturdays.
Potato-digging day was one.

I don't know why
but every year it seemed to me
Dad picked some cold wet Saturday
to tell us kids it was the perfect day
to dig the spuds we'd planted in the spring.
There wasn't anything I hated worse.
Each of us—three boys, two men—
would grab a digging fork and beat-up pail
and climb aboard the old spring wagon
            used for hauling in the load.

The patch we headed for
occupied one corner of an eighty-acre field
            that otherwise grew corn.
An oblong plot.
Its thirty rows stretched out two hundred feet.
One could figure out
how many hills we had to dig.
There were a lot.
I never took the time to make a count.
It would have made the task
            more boring than it was.

A person didn't need to know an art
        or have much skill
                or be just awfully smart
                        to dig potatoes
                                from a hill.
You simply took a digging fork in hand
and jabbed it down about as far as it would go.
Then you pulled the handle back a bit
                        to loosen up the ground
and gave a mighty heave
to turn the forkful upside down.
You stooped and picked the loot up one by one
and put it in the battered pail.
Another hill.
Fork down. Pull back. Then lift and turn.
        Stoop down. Pick up. Move on.
Fork down. Pull back. Then lift and turn.
        Stoop down. Pick up. Move on.
Hill after hill after hill.

Well that's enough of that.
Good reason anyway why digging spuds
didn't rate too high with me
                when I was growing up.

Winter

There is no sun.
The earth and sky are one.
The world has now become a giant cave.
A haven for the howling wind
that drives the falling snow in rage.

Winter

Weeks earlier
fall started leaving messages about
        hinting of her plans to leave.
Tentative at first.
Subtle in their way
yet leaving little room for doubt.

A misty trace of morning frost
              briefly seen
then lost the moment that the sun came out.

A glaze of ice
       fragile thin but clear
stretched taut across the little ponds
that once had been our footprints
        marching
            through
                the
                    yard.

Gentle orders whispered to the maple trees.
Please drop your leaves
        and let them gently fall to earth.

Signals to the blackbirds winging by
        so faint that only they could hear.
Form now in massive flights
        and try formation flying in the sky
            before you head on south.

Messages more urgent now.
All pretense gone.

Flecks of early morning snow
trace patterns on the ground.

Trees stand tall with arms outstretched.
Undressed.
Proud of their naked grace.
Adorned with only nests the robins left.

From somewhere in the north
a biting wind sweeps down

and cuts across my face to take my breath
as I walk to the barn for morning chores.

That's how it was
when fall departed from the scene
and winter came
when I was growing up.

Winter skies so much a part of every mood.
Dark now and sullen grey.
Brooding.
Closing in the earth below in loneliness.

The sky another day.
Sun washed and brilliant blue.
Reflecting glittering diamonds in the snow.

The sky at night.
A heaven with a million stars
            to bless the earth.
And to the north the Milky Way
            guarding secrets of the universe.

Winter sounds.
An ever-changing symphony.
The mournful plaintive wail of wind
whipping falling snow at night
            to pile it high
        demanding all the while
            with muted sighs
its right of entry to the house.
By dawn
the wind has won its race and gone away
leaving in its place
the even louder sound of stillness.

Winter nights and winter days
the best of times in many ways
when one is young.

Snowbound

Innocent enough at first—
those first white flakes
    drifting
        down
            gently
caught briefly in the lamplight
before coming to rest
adding freshness to the snow already there.

Another inch by morning.
No more than that.
And yet
one never could be sure this time of year.
"Still snowing out," Dad says at ten.
"Getting colder, too.
The wind's picked up a bit."
Those observations made
we go upstairs to bed.

The sound sneaks through the morning dark
           and brushes sleep away.
At first
a throaty low-pitched haunting sigh
           from somewhere far away.
A pleading cry no animal would make—
           nor mortal man.
A plaintive pleading call
           demanding to be heard.
Now and then a more persistent wail
           high-pitched and weird
as though a banshee wanted in
and having failed
slipped silently away only to return again.

Awake in darkness now
I know it is the wind
that makes those mournful sounds
and shouts commands
and shakes the house with giant hands.

It is the wind.

Awake and warm
I wonder how the world will look
when morning light replaces dark.

From my window looking out
I watch the blackness slowly fade
and see the day emerge a somber shade of grey.

There is no sun.
The earth and sky are one.
The world has now become a giant cave.
A haven for the howling wind
that drives the falling snow in rage.

Up now
I dress in everything that's warm
and hurry down to join the rest
to talk of ways we'll battle back
against this storm
          that dares invade the land.

Mom has the coffee on.

There'll be no school.
We'll break a rule and breakfast first.
Morning chores will take 'till noon
and then we'll see what must be done.
We leave the kitchen's warm and move outside.
We lean against the howling gale
that slaps each face with cold
and threatens to withhold the air we breathe
          until we reach the safety of the barn.

All day the battle rages on.
A crazy rhythm.
Advance. Retreat. Advance again.
Then rest.
And then advance once more
until by supper time
we settle for a draw.
Now warm and safe beside the burning fire

I wonder why it is that Nature can become
a mortal enemy of man.

The light of second dawn appears.
I listen for the wind but it is gone.
I hear the crushing sound of silence
                    louder still
announcing that a winter wonderland awaits
              all white and clean and cold
with towering snow-capped mountains
where no mountains were before.

Excitement takes its hold.
No school again today for sure.
We're snowbound anyway.
The roads are blocked with six-foot drifts
                    all the way to town.
They said so on the phone.
We're at the South Pole all alone.
With luck
it may be days before the snowplow comes.
Nobody knows.
We'll get the bobsled out
                    and harness up a team.
We'll make the rounds
                to see if anyone's in need.
We'll make a pair of skis.
We'll teach the dog to pull the sled.
We'll build the biggest snow fort
                        in the world.

We'll do all that and more
        the minute we get through with chores.

The Little Pond

It was always there
at least for all the time that I was growing up.
A shallow saucer—two hundred feet across—
                    no more than that.
An imperfection in the field.
No one told me how it came to be
                    but there it was
and rightly named "The Little Pond."

In spring
it caught the rivers as they flowed
from melting snow on higher ground.
Later on
it was a reservoir for storing rain
not needed by the earth.

In summer
it became a hiding place for frogs
that crouched by day beneath the lily pads above
and then burst forth at night
with croaking songs of love.
Now and then
a pair of redwing blackbirds would agree
to build their nest among the cattail reeds.
They'd raise a family of young
and teach them how to feed
          and how to fly into a summer breeze.

Sometime in fall
it might become a nesting place
for wild ducks flying south
          lost for a moment in the night
and weary from their hectic flight.

The little pond was all those things
                    three seasons of the year.

When winter came replacing fall
its surface turned into a shining jewel
that soon became the center of my universe.

Most every day
I'd hurry home from school with plans all made.
I'd get my skates and head out to the pond
to race the wind
          and practice making figure eights.
Then came delay.
I'd find my skates.
No trouble there.
The blades were sharp enough.
The leather straps okay.
But as a rule
I'd have to search all over everywhere
                to find the missing key.
We didn't have the fancy kind of skates
                    kids have today
with sharp steel blades
that fasten to those high-lace shoes
so all you have to do
is slip them on and lace them tight
and that is that.
The skates we used
clamped on whatever shoes we wore.
But as I said before
you had to have the turning key
and it was almost never in the place
where logic said it ought to be.

In any case
once at the pond with skates clamped on
my world became a magic place
of cold and wind and flashing blades
that let me trace ghost patterns on the ice.

I'd race the clock around the circle ring
                    five times or ten
and then I'd brake
to make a spray of feathered ice fan out
to catch the sun, then fall again.
I'd hide my hands behind my back
and take long sweeping strides
the way I'd seen some famous skaters do.

And when I tired of that
I'd try some fancy skating stuff
like on one leg or in reverse
until my weary ankles said enough.

At night
the pond was lighted by the moon
and we could skate in quiet cold
beneath a canopy of stars
and wonder at the beauty of it all.

On Saturdays
the neighbor kids would come.
We'd choose up sides and turn the patch of ice
                    into a perfect hockey place.
No matter that we made by hand
our crooked hockey clubs.
or that a beaten up tin can
became the focus of our battle plans.
We played to win
no matter what the cost in battered shins
                    and skinned up knees.
But if we lost
there'd always be a second chance
next Saturday.

Winter Wash Day

Wash day came on Monday during the winter—
the same as other seasons of the year.
And yet there were important differences
I can't forget when I look back.

The same routine inside of sorting clothes
          and heating water on the stove.
But temperatures outside
might register at ten below
              or colder still.
I guess the boiling water in the tubs
might warm the wash house up a bit
          say five degrees or so
but cold enough in any case
to make your face feel numb
and cold enough so even Mom
would put a heavy sweater on.

She'd drink a cup of coffee scalding hot
and dash out through the kitchen door
into the wash house filled with steam.
She'd run the first load through
that wash and rinse and wringer roll routine
         until she filled her basket to the top.

That done
she'd stop once more inside the kitchen door
to warm her hands
         and drink another cup of bitter brew
before she ventured out again.
She'd wade through foot-deep snow
to hang her dripping load of clothes
along the frigid wire lines
that ran down toward the road.

Almost before she finished with the load
the biting cold would grab ahold
and freeze each dripping piece
         stiffer than a board.

By ten o'clock or so
a passer-by would see
three ghost-like rigid rows of clothes
          freeze-drying underneath a winter sky.
The overalls hung there
          rigid straight and soldier tall
facing modestly ahead lest they observe
the funniest sight of all—
          those ghosts of long john underwear
          with buttons down the front
                    and drop-seat rears
that stood on tiptoe just above the snow.

When evening came
we'd pile the slabs of frozen clothes
across our coaster sled
                    for transport to the house.
Once there
the best part of the day would soon begin
although it may seem strange to think that way.

We knew the ritual by heart.
As soon as Mom got supper dishes done
she'd take a ball of heavy twine
and run her inside drying lines
          back and forth
                    from room
                              to room
                                        and back again
and there she hung
the still-damp clothes to dry.

One can't go home again.
We all know that.
But if I could
I'd choose a winter wash-day night
to sit beside a glowing stove
                    in dreamy lamplit quietness
and breathe the fresh clean kind of smell
that only comes from drying clothes.

The Hunter

When I was young
I used a Daisy BB gun to hunt for game—
                in make believe of course.
I'd fill the loading tube with shot
and sneak out to the snow-filled lot
in search of deer or elk
      or maybe even buffalo.
Once there
I'd crouch behind some tree or stump
and wait for one of Dad's fat steers
to wander by and volunteer to play my game.
I'd aim my deadly piece right at his rump
                and fire away.
He wouldn't flinch or jump a lick.
He'd flick his hide a bit and walk away.
But in my eye
I'd see him crumple to his knees and fall
a stricken victim of my marksmanship.

Later on my gun became a .22.
It was an ancient single shot
Dad bought at some farm auction sale
              for shooting rats.
With that fine piece I changed the game.
I became a lawman of the West instead.
Sent out alone
I'd bring a gambling killer home
where he'd stand trial
      and then would hang 'till dead.
I'd sharpen up my shooting skill
by placing tin cans in a row
and drilling them with rifle holes
            one at a time.
I'd practice tracking in the snow
until there was no way I'd fail
to find my hunted man
and make him pay the final price for crime.

But in the process of all this
I graduated in the art of using guns
and started killing living things
just for the fun of it.
I knew in truth
there were no deer or buffalo around the farm.
And I was not about to face a killer on the loose
        no matter what my fantasy might show.
But there were crows in flight
and rabbits running in the snow

and quail to find
and ring-necked pheasants we might shoot
      before they winged away in flight.

It's true
a small boy with a .22
can't hit too many moving things
and so my body count of fallen game was low.
Mostly I just hunted for the fun of it
until the .410 shotgun came along
and changed the odds
      in favor of the one who held the gun.

I'd wait until there'd been fresh snow.
Then after morning chores I'd dress up warm
and stuff my pockets full of shells
to head out for the open fields
      and be a hunter for a day.

Most of the time
I had the friendly cottontail in mind.
He used the night for playing games.
He'd scamper through the snow
leaving lines of crooked trails
that I could track when morning came.
Once I saw him in his hiding place
I'd challenge him to run
and play a deadly racing game—
his frightened darting speed
against the swiftness of my gun.
The moment he took off in fear
I'd take quick aim
and squeeze the trigger tight.
I'd hear the blast exploding in my ear
and see him spin around in death.
I'd be a little out of breath
but I would know my gun had won again.

Somehow in memory now
I wonder why
      when I was growing up
I found such fun in hunting with a gun.

Butchering

I'd turn my back
but I'd still hear that rifle crack
and know
      there in the driveway of the crib
that Dad had shot the pig behind the ear.
Once stunned
      as Mom explained one day
the animal would feel no pain
and have no fear of harm
when Dad took out his sticking knife
and slit its throat
to let its life blood flow away
             dark red and warm.
Even so
I never cared too much to see it done
although the rest of butchering was fun
      when I was growing up.

The afternoon before
Dad picked the one to pay the final price.
We penned it in the crib
until the crucial time to sacrifice its life.

Now in the early morning sun
we'd fill a fifty-gallon drum half full
and underneath
we'd build a raging fire with cobs
to heat the water boiling hot.
Then with a block-and-tackle rig
we'd hoist the carcass of the pig up high
and lower it head down again
to scald it in the steaming vat.
We did that once or twice
so that our sharpened butcher knives
could scrape those bristles off the hide
            in nothing flat.

That done
the rest of us stepped back
and watched Dad demonstrate his art.

He'd make one slashing stroke
to slit the carcass stem to stern
and then
he'd reach his hand inside the opening
and place the heart and liver in a pail
for us to take to Mom.
Intestines next were taken out
and saved for sausage casings later on.
The other inside stuff
was buried out behind the barn.

After that Dad split the carcass head to tail
        leaving two pale sides of pork
        for him to work his magic on.
He'd take one side a time
and lay it on his butcher's block
        fashioned out of heavy planks
                twelve inches wide.
With cutting saw and knives honed razor sharp
he'd transform what had been a pig
        into its various parts.
There'd be bacon slabs and huge red hams
        and cuts of shoulder meat
                to cure with hickory smoke.
There'd be spareribs lean and tenderloins
        that Mom would can in mason jars.
Without a backward glance
                he'd toss into a heavy tub
                all odds and ends that we would use
for grinding sausage some night soon.
He'd fill another tub with fat
for melting down to render lard.
It was a fascinating show
        the way Dad worked.
He'd finished butchering by noon
and we could think about the other tasks
        still waiting to be done.

The Sausage Makers

Making sausage had the most appeal—
                for me at any rate.

174

We'd stay up late
and make a little ceremony out of it.
The kitchen turned into the sausage-making room
            as soon as Mom got supper dishes done.

At station one
the brooding Buddha of a sausage press
squatted on the table top
            its feet clamped down
waiting for someone to feed it meat
            and twist its arm
so it could spew it forth again.

At station two
there'd be a tub of small intestines
            soaking in a salty brine
ready to be lifted out and scraped and scrubbed
atop a bed slat borrowed for the night.

The members of another crew
had full command of station three.
There with sharpened knives in hand
they'd cut the meat to bite-sized bits
and let the sausage grinder chew them up
before it spit them out again into a holding pan
where Mom would blend the seasoning in.

The lamps burn bright.
The crews are set to go.
Fill the waiting press with meat
and tie a casing end up tight
            around the iron exit spout.
Now turn the crank real slow
and force the meat to flow into the casing skin
            to form a giant sausage snake
                some two feet long or so.
Tie a string around both ends and set aside.
Attach another casing skin.
Bring on more meat.
Refill the press and turn the crank
until another slithering snake is born
            and then another one
                until you're done.

The Lard Maker

Next morning as a rule
Mom took the fat Dad saved and rendered lard.
Before we left for school
we'd prop the big old iron kettle on some stones
                              out in the yard
and start a roaring fire underneath
with cobs and coal and sawed-off two by fours.
Mom would cut the fat in chunks
        about the size of eggs I guess
        and toss the whole mess in the vat
        to cook all day.

From time to time
        she'd stir the bubbling brew
        and give the fire a poke or two.
By night
the grease had all boiled out
        and risen to the top.
The bits of lean had cooked dark brown
        and fallen to the bottom of the pot.
When that time came
Mom took some gallon syrup tins
and filled each to the brim
with amber grease in liquid form
        that slowly hardened into lard
        for use all winter long.

The Soap Maker

Next day
Mom used the same black iron pot
for making soap.
First thing
she'd fix a wicked broth
of water mixed with store-bought lye
that came in scary cans
        with skulls and crossbones on their sides.
She knew it took ten pounds of grease
for every quart of potent brew.

176

The grease was mostly leavings from the lard
stretched out with other grease she'd saved
                    in old glass mason jars.
She'd mix the whole conglomeration in the pot
and let it boil until it got just right for
pouring into shallow pans to harden overnight.
Then she'd take a paring knife
and cut the soap in square-shaped cakes
                    for washing clothes.

I guess that pig would never know
how many things he meant to us.

Winter Morning

Morning light.
Grey. Ghostlike. Cold.
Filtered from night's dark shades.
Holding back the day.
Reluctant and indifferent.
Promising little.
Bitter from the sun's neglect and hostile
but slowly giving way.

Morning sounds.
Sharp against the muffled stillness.
Distinct. Penetrating. Insistent.
Carried by the cold—
        demanding to be heard.
The barn.
Warm. Sweet smelling. Safe.
Haven from the cold.
Soft filtered light.
Low stifled sounds.
Animals awake—polite but restless
                waiting now for men to come.
The silo.
Frigid feed-filled tower tube.
Defiant and alone.
Taller than the barn.
Daring man to scale its side
and find inside
        a cave of howling winds.

The windmill.
Gaunt skeleton of steel
            standing guard.
Fan-shaped face now still.
Immobilized
'till man will turn it to the wind
                and set it free.

The crib.
Twin vaults of slatted boards

                    painted red
containing yellow gold called corn
                    for feeding steers.
Up above
gigantic boxes holding oats
          flowing on demand through wooden chutes.

Images.
Grey smoke curling upward in the cold.
          White misty breath exhaled.
                    Sheltered drifts of snow.
                    Fresh rabbit tracks.
Moving shadows from the lantern's light.
A night owl going home.
A winter morning on a farm.
A world alone.

Garden Center Christmas Program

Murmuring voices fade.
A quiet hush invades the room.
It now becomes
       a center for performing arts.

Three borrowed muslin sheets
       starched fresh and ironed smooth
united now as one with safety pins
curtain off from view the center stage.

The house is packed.
The audience awaits.
Proud parents all in gingham gowns and overalls
       sit beneath red streamers made of crepe.

Out in the hall
       beside the hanging coats and caps
the cast of famous acting stars
silently rehearse their lines
       and dry their sweaty hands.

The time has come.
No turning back.
Inside the house lights dim
       as borrowed lamps are turned down low.
The actors put aside their fright.
The Garden Center Christmas program now begins
with sixteen off-key voices singing
       "Silent Night."

Men of the Road

Some claimed
they left signs when they went away.
Signs on a post somewhere along the road
          or down by the driveway gate.
Signs telling others who followed
how they rated the place
in terms of food and shelter and kindness
          and whether or not the dog would bite.

We looked for signs like that.
Never found them.
Yet there must have been something
to cause wandering men of the road
               to rate our place so highly.

They always stopped at dusk
          when it was cold
                    and we were doing chores.
Perhaps the warm lamplight
coming from the kitchen window
reminded them of a home they once knew
before they became no one
               going nowhere.
People called them tramps
          or hobos
                    or bums.
Some said they were good men
               down on their luck.
Others said they were shiftless no-accounts
                    who didn't want to work.
No one really knew.

Mom always fixed a supper plate
and had them eat in the little kitchen
                    where it was warm.
Afterwards they would sleep in the barn
               leaving at dawn
and we would never see them again.

That bothered me.

Garden Center Box Social

Now gentlemen
I tell you what we're gonna do.
We're gonna start this auction off
                        right here and now.
So get your money out and listen to the rules.

These lovely ladies here
            you know them all
                        and bless their hearts
each one has worked real hard
to fix a lot of dandy food
and decorate a box all nice to put it in.
They've done their part and more
                        I'll tell you that
and now they want to see if you can do as well.

What I'm gonna do is this.
I'm gonna start each box at fifty cents.
That's right—a half a buck
            and go on up from there.
The highest bidder gets the box and more.
He gets the gal who brung it
as his partner for the night
            so long as she is not his wife
                        you understand.

Okay we'll start right off with number one.
A beauty of a thing—all pink and ribbon tied.
Who bids it off at fifty cents?
I have it there from Ralph.
Now who gives seventy-five?

Excitement mounts with every bid.
The men all grin and kid a lot
and look around the room
to see if they can figure out
            which box belongs to whom
and most of all
which one the teacher brought.

Us boys will do the same
when our turn comes to play the game and
bid on boxes that the girls have fixed.

Outside
bitter wind blows cold
and snowdrifts start to curl across the yard.
But no one cares.
Inside
it's bright and warm with fun
and every person old and young
has waited for this night
        that makes the winter seem less cruel—
box social night at Garden Center School.

The Christmas Season

The Revelation

Some modern parents think it wrong
to let kids when they're young
believe in Santa Claus
and then reveal the truth a little later on.
I don't know the pros and cons of that.
But I believed in old Saint Nick
     when I was growing up
and never thought it did much harm.
I even thought it sort of fun
when I found out that Santa Claus
     was really Dad and Mom.
Here's how it came about.

My older brother
   wiser for his extra years
told me he could prove his case
since I was filled with doubt.
So once we went to bed on Christmas Eve
     we stayed awake.
Then like quiet elves
we saw the truth unfold below
   as we watched through the chimney grate.
In actual fact
we played the pretend game an extra year.
We wanted Mom and Dad to have the fun
     of playing Santa Claus.

The Dream Book

Wind-up trains complete with tracks.
Cowboy suits with leather chaps.
Model cars and gopher traps.
Erector sets and Tinkertoys.
Tops that spin like gyroscopes.
Fancy saddles for the pony.
Indian bows with twenty arrows.
Pocket knives and fancy watches.

Horseshoe sets and two-head axes.
Flyer sleds and coaster wagons.
Frontier forts you build with matches.
Stocking caps and matching jackets.
Magic sets and pencil boxes.

The fire glows.
Stretched out on the floor
        I lie there warm
                and dream my Christmas dream.
If only everything were free
        as offered in the catalog
put out by Sears Roebuck and Company.

Mom's Christmas Candy

Rich and full bodied
        languid and sensuous
dusky brown from a thousand suns
tempting with fragrance of other lands
        sweet chocolate
                the essence of vanilla
hot blooded and indolent
moving indifferently into the shallow pan
                        to cool.
The first full batch of fudge is done.
Mom lets us lick the pan.

Prim and proper
        like young girls at their first dance
all alike in white dresses
        innocent and shy
sitting politely in straight rows
waiting
offering sugar-sweet temptation
hidden now in coolness
        behind closed parlor doors.
We have to wait 'till Christmas Day
to have these lovely maidens of divinity
                that Mom has made.

Christmas Eve

No night could be more special
     more filled with warmth
          more touched with cheer
more vividly remembered now for special things.
Snow creaking in the cold
          as we do chores.
First night stars
     soon joined by millions more
the way it must have been that night
          so long ago.

The kitchen filled with lamplight.
The table set.
The menu just the same
as all the other Christmas Eves before
     and all the ones we'd ever know.
A giant kettle warms atop the kitchen range
     filled half with milk and half with cream
soon joined by oysters Mom pours in
     at least a quart or two
for feasting Christmas Eve on oyster stew.

Hurry now to dress in Sunday best.
The program starts at eight.
We'll miss the Christmas carols if we're late.
The ride to town.
A winter wonderland of falling snow.
We're there.
Everybody stamps their feet
so not to track the damp inside.

From up in front
a mammoth Christmas tree surveys the scene.
Its branches laced with tinsel strands
     and bright red paper chains
and ornaments of every kind
     made by the Ladies Aid.
There's murmured neighbor talk
about those things that neighbors talk about.

The program is about to start.
The church is filled with muffled quietness.
The curtains part to show the manger scene.
Three wise men walk onto the stage.
They're boys we know
            in costumes that their mothers made.
They're joined by little angels dressed in white.
All speak their lines
            and then depart relieved.
Their places taken turn by turn
            by others chosen to recite.

The curtains close again.
The program's over for the night.
We wait for what we know will come.
The sound of sleigh bells drawing near.
And then a loud commotion at the door.
A hearty ho ho laugh
and sure enough
there's someone all dressed up like Santa Claus.
The younger kids are sort of scared.
The older ones all think they know
it's neighbor Anderson
            with pillows front and rear.
How can they be so sure?
He stops and asks each one if he's been good.
And when the answer's yes
he reaches in his bag
and fishes out a small brown paper bag
filled to the top
with cheap rock Christmas candy.
How could there be in all the world
a nicer gift than that.

The snow has stopped.
The night is colder still.
As we drive home this silent night
there truly is a peace on earth—
            or so at least it seemed
            when we were growing up.

Christmas Morning

Still dark with night inside our room.
I am awake.
I pull the curtain back and peer outside.
The stars are there
      as bright as when we went to bed.
And yet I'm sure the sky is lighter
                in the east.
It is a subtle kind of lightness
                only boys can see
when morning comes to Christmas Day.

I lie there warm and wait.
A teasing pleasure in delay.
My mind plays guessing games.
What will I find when I dash down
      dressed only in my underwear?
There are so many things I've dreamed about.

My brothers move.
They are awake.
We softly talk.
We say we'll wait 'till each one counts
five hundred times real fast
and then we'll make a dash downstairs.
My turn comes last.
I reach four hundred ninety-nine.
With that we toss the covers back and run.
No time to light the lamp
      and anyway it's lighter out.
I see it there
      beneath the stocking with my name.
A giant cardboard box.
I shout out loud.
My heart begins to pound.
I know inside that box
I'll find a brand new wind-up train
      with twenty feet of track.
The dream I dared to dream came true.
Santa Claus is real
      regardless of his honest name.

Christmas Day

Chores got done on Christmas Day
      same as any other day I guess.
Cows got milked and cattle fed.
Barns got cleaned and all the rest.
Those things are hazy in my mind.
I find a lot of other things
much easier to recall.

We set the train track up
and ran my train around the figure eight
        at least a hundred times.
We coasted on the Flyer sled
      my little brother got
and shot my older brother's .22.

We tried on brand-new stocking caps
        and skated on the pond.
We hitched the horses to the sleigh
and drove to see the Wilson boys
to try out all the gifts they got.

Sometime in early afternoon we headed home
and helped Mom get the Christmas dinner on.
We ate until there wasn't room for more.
Then we pulled our chairs up to the stove
and talked or took a little snooze
until Dad roused us out to help with chores.

That's how it was on Christmas Day.